Contents

Acknowledgements

With thanks to Dr Richard Woolfson, chartered educational psychologist.

Special thanks also to Emma Shackleton for commissioning the book!

Introduction

Welcome to the only source of information you should need to help you make the right childcare choice for your family. I can remember very clearly the bewilderment and apprehension I felt when faced with finding childcare for my baby. I hadn't anticipated that I would need to take this route, working as I did from home as a freelance writer. Instead I'd had misty-eyed visions of typing away contentedly for hours on end, my newborn sleeping peacefully next to me in her Moses basket. In reality she slept fitfully and in short bursts, and she spent a good deal of her waking hours screaming with colic, all of which meant that for the first few months of her life I became a full-on, full-time mum, and work went out the window.

After the colic abated, when Natasha was about 16 weeks old, new challenges took over: my baby was no longer a newborn and seemed to develop new curiosities and make ever more demands on me daily. I loved our one-to-one time together and would happily have continued as her full-time carer until she was ready for her pre-school nursery place at age three, but we'd known when we made the decision to start a family that we wouldn't be able to survive on one salary alone, and that was that.

Because I needed to keep working, childcare became inevitable, but I felt as if I had a mountain to climb before it would all be sorted out. What were my options? How would I know what was right for my baby? Who else could possibly understand her needs? Where exactly were these childminders and nurseries I needed to investigate? How long were the waiting lists? What was it all going to cost? How would I make it work for all the family? My long experience of writing parenting articles did nothing to prepare me for the search ahead – but it did enable me to identify a real need for a comprehensive guide to choosing childcare!

There's a lot more to finding the right childcare than just identifying who can mind your child and for how long at a time: as a parent your first concern will be to find a carer you can trust; you will need to be sure of your child's safety and will probably want to maintain some control over his day-to-day upbringing; you'll be keen to ensure that he is stimulated and encouraged to develop at a rate appropriate to his age. This book will guide you through each step of the process and enable you to make a choice with which both you and your child are happy.

Hilary Pereira

Author's note: I have opted to refer to children alternately as 'he' or 'she' from chapter to chapter. This makes for easier reading than stating 'him/her', 'his/her' or 'he/she' in each instance. For the same reason I also refer to 'mums' instead of 'mums/dads', although I am happy to say that more dads than ever before are taking on childcare.

Chapter 1

Why are you considering childcare?

If, like most parents, you have qualms about putting your child in someone else's care, the guidance contained within these pages – backed up by research and expert advice – will help to allay them. Before you start reading in earnest, here's some great news to have come out of the research: studies show that good-quality, well-chosen childcare can have a very positive effect on children, both socially and intellectually (a fact that is examined in more detail in the next chapter and throughout the book).

First things first: let's examine the reasons why you are considering childcare for your baby or child. For some parents it's a question of the need to earn money; for others it's a matter of personal fulfilment; for some, it's the conviction that pre-school daycare will give their children a head start for school; for others it's to provide a temporary reprieve from full-time parenting – and for many families, it's a complex mix of some or all of the above.

Financial necessity

In many families both parents are forced back to work in order to make ends meet. For these families the decision whether or not to use childcare is already made because financial necessity outweighs the inevitable burden of childcare costs – unless, of course, they fall into the category whose family or friends can provide childminding facilities for free or for a minimal cost (see page 77). Understandably, most families would prefer a choice as to whether or not they use childcare. A recent survey of 4,000 working parents found that 88% of mums in full-time jobs would prefer to work part time or stay at home full time with their children, but can't make the change because they need to bring in a full-time salary.

This finding is borne out by researchers for the government's National Childcare Strategy who found, during the course of their study into Childcare and Early Years Provision, that for 36% of families who use childcare, money was the motivating factor. It can be a double-edged sword: both parents need to work in order to boost family finances, but a great deal of income is automatically cancelled out by the cost of childcare.

Despite the government now providing free childcare for all children from age three to starting school, for many working families arrangements will have to be in place from when their babies are infants, and – unless they can rely at least in part on the unpaid support of friends and family, or are eligible for benefits such as Working Tax Credit to help with the cost of childcare (see Chapter 8) – this will prove to be a costly business.

Whether you're returning to work and your working hours overlap with your partner's, or you're currently unemployed but want or need to find a job, or you're retraining to get back to work, you'll need to have reliable childcare – and fall-back arrangements, if possible – in place.

> *'I was hoping we'd be able to tighten our belts sufficiently after Beth was born for me to stay home with her until she went to school. I thought that with the money I was saving on travel, lunches and after-work socialising, we'd manage on Alan's salary alone, but I'd underestimated just how much of the family income goes on essentials like nappies, formula milk and clothes. Although I didn't have my usual daily outgoings, the fact that I was at home all day meant the fuel and food bills increased, too – and so did the telephone and internet bills, as I was quite bored. In the end I was forced to return to work part time. Even though it doesn't make a huge financial difference, that bit extra takes the strain off Alan – and I'm less bored than I was at home, too.'*
>
> Esther, 33, mum to Beth, 10 months

Rising fees of private nurseries

According to a survey by Daycare Trust, the national childcare charity, a typical full-time private nursery place for a child under two in the UK currently costs £142 a week – the equivalent of over £7,300 a year. With last year's average earnings standing at £447 a week, this means that for some families a nursery place could account for up to a third of their income. Private nursery places in London and the southeast are by far the most costly, with some parents forking out almost £21,000 a year.

Personal fulfilment or career progression

One of the worries new parents voice is that failure to return to work promptly will cost them their position and career prospects for the future. One answer could be to take a 'career break' – a predetermined period of unpaid leave, after which time you return to your job at your previous level of seniority. This, though, is only an option for families who can afford to drop one salary for the duration of the career break – and it's not just the family income that suffers: you will also lose other benefits, such as 'death-in-service' payout, unless you arrange alternative cover through your own insurance company, and your employer's contributions to your pension and National Insurance will cease whilst you are away from work.

For all these reasons, many mums decide to go back to work, whether full or part time – some before they have the desire to do so. Amongst those who return full time, many cite the fact that part-timers are not always treated as equals: they are sometimes excluded from workplace briefings; they're passed over for promotion; they're often missed off social invitation lists and are not valued as highly as full-timers. Amongst those who go back to work part time, many give their reasons as being financial (they can't afford full-time childcare) or sacrificial (they are giving up earnings and position because, although they value their career, they also want to spend time at home with their children).

There are also mothers who choose to make childcare arrangements regardless of their own work commitments, and some employ carers despite not working themselves at all. For these women, retaining a sense of their own individuality is as important as the role of new motherhood: they may resent being regarded more as the mothers of their children than as people in their own right. This group of mothers believes that social interaction with other adults, 'me' time and other time spent away from their babies makes them more effective as parents.

Some families choose for both partners to work because the extra income can finance luxuries such as family holidays, a new car, a larger house or the latest home entertainment products, without which the job of parenting would feel like too much of a sacrifice.

What mums say about why they chose childcare

'After two months of visitors directing all their questions and attentions towards Alana and failing to ask me anything about myself, I decided that if I didn't claw some of my old life back I'd go mad. I discussed it with my husband, Peter, and we decided that I should have two days a week to myself to catch up with friends, go swimming or just relax on my own. Our local nursery would only take Alana for a minimum of four half days or two whole days, so we chose the second option: neither of us wanted to burden our own mums with a whole day's childcare every week. The nursery fees are expensive, especially as I don't work, but they're worth every penny. Now, on the days I spend with Alana, I feel like a much better mummy.'

Deonne, 28, mum to Alana, six months

'I had no doubt when I went on maternity leave that I would be back at the helm of my job as soon as it was over. As a team manager for a major bank, I run a team of 25 staff and I love my job. I actually really missed work whilst I was off! I knew I'd never be happy as a full-time mum, and as I'm the main breadwinner in our household it wouldn't be practical anyway. My sister has two children, both of whom went to a childminder and thrived on the care: they're both well-balanced, clever kids who have no problems socialising. What's been good enough for them is good enough for Matthew, too. He's been going to his childminder for four months now and is completely happy as far as I'm concerned. Yes, it costs a lot – but we're still better off than we would be otherwise, and I wouldn't want things any other way.'

Adriana, 33, mum to Matthew, 10 months

'Although my boss said that I would be offered a job on the same salary scale as before whenever I chose to go back, I knew that she would move me to a department she knows I don't enjoy if I took extended maternity leave. She's been known to do this before to try to get part-timers to resign – and she's very clever about it because she always manages to stay within the constraints of employment law. I called her bluff by going back on the first day after my maternity leave ended, although I'd prefer not to be working at all, to be honest. My mum and auntie are looking after the twins between them, though, so at least I've got free childcare.'

Hayley, 36, mum to Jenna and Jordan, seven months

'Because I've always earned more than my partner, my salary is crucial to us as a family, so we've swapped roles and David is part-time carer to Dylan. David's still working as an estate agent, and we're not planning more children because David doesn't want to be out of the job market for an extended period. We've found a great childminder whom Dylan adores. She has him three days a week while David works. I get to keep my position as a marketing manager in a publishing company and all the perks that brings with it, and I'm happy knowing that Dylan is being well cared for by his childminder and his dad. I think we're really lucky.'

Melinda, 26, mum to Dylan, 11 months

A head start for school

Research conducted by the National Audit Office (NAO) into the reasons why families use childcare found that 43% of parents cited social interaction with other children as being of greatest perceived benefit to their children, and this has certainly been proven in studies involving three- to five-year-olds. Since the introduction of the government Sure Start programme's Early Years Foundation Stage frameworks, providing education targets for babies up to five-year-olds, some parents also feel that their children can gain greater educational benefit from taking up a free childcare place than from what they can offer at home. In other words, these parents feel under-qualified to begin educating their children effectively themselves.

Sure Start's Effective Provision of Pre-school Education (EPPE) project, which assessed the impact of different types of pre-school care on children up to age seven, concurred in part with this idea (see page 28). According to its findings, published in November 2004, babies and children who attended some sort of formal pre-school group achieved more in terms of cognitive development than children who experienced only home-based care. Children who were cared for at home remained at a 'significant disadvantage' throughout Key Stage 1 and up to age seven, according to the report, and this was after taking into account the children's different backgrounds, parents, carers and home environments.

> *'Eli was born curious and always seemed a couple of steps ahead of other babies his age in his mental development. I just didn't feel like I was the right person to get the best out of him, especially as he got bored with his toys very quickly and wasn't a baby who liked to sit in front of a video. A friend whose baby attended a very good private nursery took me along to introduce myself and Eli. The babies were doing so much stimulating stuff that I just knew it would be great for him. I've done the opposite of what most mums do: I've gone back to work so I can afford for Eli to go to nursery. I don't really make any money once I've paid the fees, but he's coming on brilliantly and has made lots of new friends, so I don't mind.'*
>
> Eva, single mum to Eli, 14 months

Better social skills

Babies and children who are generally clingy or reticent about mixing with other adults and children sometimes benefit from short periods of childcare – whether in a formal setting or as time spent with other family members or friends. In some cases, it brings them out of their shell and helps them to socialise, as well as encouraging particular skills such as sharing, teamwork and problem solving.

Good childcare can build confidence in babies and self-esteem in young children, and the inherent routines can engender a sense of wellbeing and security. It can also encourage infants who are naturally gregarious to express and maintain the sociable side of their personalities, as well as giving them great opportunities to make friends and learn new skills.

If you're unsure whether or not your child will take to separation from you, it's probably best to start by leaving him for a short time (say, an hour) with someone he knows, trusts and – if possible – loves. It's equally important that the person you have chosen has a special bond with him, as their care will be closest to what you can offer yourself.

It's certainly worth avoiding the window of difficult, super-clingy behaviour, which often begins between seven and nine months, as a starting point for separation. This is the time when many babies refuse to let their mums out of their sight – a phase of development commonly known as 'separation anxiety' (also discussed on pages 159–61). Better to start childcare ahead of this period or delay it until your baby is closer to his first birthday or seems to have got over his clinginess.

> *'I found a childminder a month before we needed one, and began making short visits with Aiden so they could get acquainted. Aiden was six months old at the time and seemed more than happy with Elaine. But as the time drew nearer for the childcare to start properly, his behaviour changed completely. Suddenly he'd scream the place down if I left the room without taking him with me. Each time I took him to Elaine's he'd go rigid and hysterical when I tried to leave. Elaine said he'd probably be fine once I'd gone, but it was so out of character that I couldn't have left him like that, so I had to give up his place. Aiden got over this phase when he was about 10 months old, but Elaine isn't available at the moment and I still haven't found a childminder I really like. Luckily, my mum and mother-in-law have agreed to share the care between them until I find someone new.'*
>
> Lizzie, mum to Aiden, 13 months

When to start looking

Many parents are confused as to when they should start researching childcare options. The answer is that once you know you are pregnant, it's never too early, and it's certainly wise to begin by the time you reach the beginning of your second trimester of pregnancy. Just like choosing a school, selecting childcare should be given top priority – and it's just as important as school selection, because your baby's early experiences will all play a part in his future wellbeing and character development. It stands to reason that starting early will serve you well, as the best childcare providers – unless they are only recently established – will inevitably have the longest waiting lists.

Even if you're not planning on using a childcare place for many months after the birth of your baby, your situation or circumstances may change between now and then, and it will be just as well to have something to fall back on: you can always cancel a place if you don't need it – and, if the provider is renowned, there will be someone lined up and waiting for that place – but if you leave it too late, you will have very little scope for finding childcare and may have to settle for a provider who may not have been your first choice.

Another plus to starting your childcare search early in pregnancy is that you will have time to make a leisurely appraisal of each of your local providers, visiting at least twice at times that are convenient to you. You'll also have more time for reflection between visits, and this could give rise to more questions for you to ask at your next drop in.

Bear in mind, too, that a good nanny who is currently employed will probably be required by her current employer to give a month's notice before leaving. Childminders usually don't want to commit too far in advance, but may agree to keeping a place open for you if you pay a retaining fee.

Chapter 2

Why the right childcare is a good thing

It's official: good childcare can be of great benefit to infants and parents alike. Children who have experienced high-quality pre-school care often gain a head start over their stay-at-home peers in terms of intellectual and social development – a fact that is borne out by several high-profile research studies (see page 28). However, not all publicity seems to concur: one of the biggest international studies of recent times, carried out by the National Institute of Child Health and Human Development in the USA, suggested that 'the more time children spent in childcare from birth to age four and a half, the more adults tended to rate them as less likely to get along with others; as more assertive, as disobedient and as aggressive'. Within the results, published in July 2003, the authors did concede, however, that 'for the vast majority of children, the levels of the behaviours reported were well within the normal range'. The study has its critics who argue that because the work was started in 1991 before all formal forms of childcare became more stringently regulated, the findings are no longer relevant, especially in the UK.

'Good-quality childcare, when delivered by qualified and trained staff who follow a planned programme of stimulation, can add a new dimension to a young child's life: the stimulation of a dynamic childcare placement can significantly boost all aspects of development,' says chartered educational psychologist Dr Richard Woolfson. 'Complementing what a child's parents already provide, a new range of activities, challenges and social experiences in childcare can consolidate and extend learning, language skills, physical skills and social skills.'

Whether or not we feel that childcare is ultimately to the greater benefit or detriment of our children, the fact remains for many families that keeping children at home until primary school age, or at least deferring childcare for the first year, as advocated by some experts, are options that are simply not feasible. It costs, according to a new survey conducted by TV channel Discovery Home & Health, around £164,000 to raise a child from birth to university, so it's hardly surprising that over 40% of mothers in Britain return to work before their babies' first birthday. Despite the fact that what's left over after paying childcare costs is often very little – depending on what arrangements are in place – for some families it can make the difference between balancing the books or falling into debt, or enjoying luxuries such as family holidays and upgrades to home comforts.

What is childcare?

There are various types of registered and unregistered childcare on offer: for now, we'll be focusing first and foremost on registered childcare; unregistered provision, such as that offered by friends and family, nannies and au pairs, will be examined in Chapters 3 and 4, as well as elsewhere in the book.

Registered childcare includes nurseries, pre-schools, playgroups, childminders, out-of-school provision and Sure Start Children's Centres. The term 'full daycare' refers to facilities that provide daycare for children up to the age of eight for a continuous period of four hours or more in any day on premises other than domestic: for example, day nurseries and Children's Centres.

The regulation of the various forms of childcare and pre-school provision in the UK has historically been divided between the Department of Health (covering children from birth to age three) and the Department of Education (responsible for children from age three to school-joining age). Nowadays, however, responsibility for childcare for all age groups – including its regulation and inspection – lies with the Sure Start unit of the Department for Education and Skills (www.surestart.gov.uk). The Sure Start unit also launched Investors in Children (IiC), which is an initiative designed to help nurseries, childminders, after-school clubs, crèches and playgroups to take part in an accredited quality assurance (QA) scheme, which is independently endorsed by its professional panel. (For a list of the QA schemes endorsed to date, and more information on what they represent, visit www.surestart.gov.uk.)

Positive childcare can mean happier children

The good news is that a recent report by a professor at the University of London's Institute for the Study of Children maintains that young children who enjoy quality childcare are happier, display better social skills with their friends and peers, show greater personal maturity and are less likely to have behavioural problems. One of the greatest benefits of good pre-school provision, according to the report, is the increased opportunity for children to develop their skills, both social and educational, alongside interaction with their peers. This interplay between same-age pre-school children, the study concluded, is becoming ever more important with the general reduction in average family size coupled with the fact of increased family mobility and other factors that have resulted in fewer opportunities for peer play in pre-schoolers.

Children who enjoy high-quality pre-school care are reportedly also better able to concentrate, better prepared for school and more likely to do well academically at age eleven. American trials back these findings up, with long term follow-up discovering evidence of increased employment, lower teenage pregnancy rates, higher social status and decreased criminal behaviour amongst these groups. There are reports, too, of positive effects on mothers' education, employment and interaction with their children – and this produces a positive knock-on effect amongst their offspring. One research project, conducted by academics at the universities of Bristol, Kent and Bath, has found that children who attend a pre-school nursery while their mothers enjoy fulfilling jobs suffer from much lower stress levels than children whose mothers have unfulfilling jobs or who are emotionally exhausted by staying home all day as full-time carers. So there's no need to feel guilty about using childcare resources that, when carefully chosen to match the needs of both you and your child, can really help enhance development, both socially and developmentally.

Characteristics of positive childcare and what the Early Years Foundation Stage offers

Positive childcare is any provision that allows children to grow, develop and explore in a safe, stimulating environment – and at an age-appropriate rate. This could be with or without other children, but should ideally include a mix of one-to-one attention as well as larger-group activities where possible. Where a parent, friend or childminder who minds only your child is concerned, these could include, for example, mother-and-toddler groups, toddler music workshops or soft-play sessions locally.

The government's Early Years Foundation Stage frameworks lay down specific areas for development amongst babies and children up to age five, and should have a positive impact, long term, on early development. One of the objectives is for all children up to school-joining age and, in the case of out-of-school provision, beyond, to gain more than just babysitting from childcare.

The frameworks have been designed to encourage children to be confident and independent, to build their self-esteem and to help them get a head start with a broad spectrum of age-appropriate learning.

Birth to three

In the early days, from birth to age three, the four specific aims that all childcarers are expected to work towards, in accordance with the 'Birth to Three Matters' curriculum, are that from baby- to toddlerhood each child will be:

- encouraged to be emotionally secure, with a strong self-identity and sense of belonging
- taught to be a skilful communicator able to share thoughts, feelings and, eventually, ideas; and to forge friendships and listen effectively
- developed into a competent learner who is able to be creative and imaginative, and to connect ideas in order to make sense of the world
- nurtured into a healthy child who is growing and developing emotionally and physically at a rate appropriate to her age.

Three to five

Onwards from age three to five, the 'Foundation Stage' is organised into six defined areas:

Personal, social and emotional development

As well as being able to dress and undress herself, your child will be further encouraged to be self-confident; to have an inquiring mind; to be able to identify her own needs and communicate them to others and to know the difference between right and wrong.

Communication, language and literacy

With the aid of stories, poems and songs, your child will learn to talk fluently and clearly. More emphasis will be placed on hearing and saying sounds accurately, and linking them to the alphabet. Manual dexterity and fine motor skills are encouraged by the introduction of basic writing skills using a pencil.

Mathematical development

Numbers and concepts such as 'bigger', 'smaller', 'over', 'under', 'heavier than' and 'lighter than' will be reinforced through stories, games, songs and role play. Shape identification and spatial awareness are also on the learning agenda for this age group.

Knowledge and understanding of the world

Exploration of the world around her through the media of textiles, construction materials and everyday technology will increase your child's perception and understanding of her surroundings. She will also be encouraged to explore her own and her family's past, and will find out more about different cultures and faiths.

Physical development

Balance, physical strength, control and confidence in her own motor skills will be encouraged through physical activity and increasingly challenging climbing equipment.

Creative development

Creativity encompassing dance, role play, music-making, story-telling and the exploration of colour, shape, light effects and texture should all be covered under the 'Foundation Stage' curriculum.

Staff qualifications

The level of qualification of childcare providers currently varies between different centres and types of provision, but one thing registered providers have in common is that they must adhere to the Early Years Foundation Stage programme. Centres offering daycare for children under the age of eight should have well-qualified managers (usually to level 3 in Childcare or Playwork, with at least two years' experience of working in a daycare setting). Other staff currently need not have formal qualifications, depending on the setting (see Chapter 3), but must have the appropriate experience, skills and ability to care for children. More information about the criteria required to reach level 3 in Childcare and Playwork is available from the Children's Workforce Development Council (see page 178).

The government has pledged help for childcare workers to study for a graduate-level qualification as Early Years Professionals. National childcare charity Daycare Trust agrees that ideally there should be a core professional trained at graduate level as a pedagogue in formal childcare settings, with around 60% of the workforce having graduate-level qualifications with salary and benefits to match. The remaining 40% of the workforce should be assistant pedagogues with at least level 3 qualifications in Childcare or Playwork. The fact that the government and the childcare sector agree that children's education is crucial from a young age and should be supported in practical terms is really encouraging for the future.

Child-led activities

As well as following the Early Years Foundation Stage curriculum, a good childcare provider will be prepared to tune in to your child's individual needs, and to plan activities and play opportunities that encourage her emotional, physical, social and educational development. There shouldn't be a 'blanket' policy for all children under the provider's care: each child's personality and preferences need to be taken into account in order for her to thrive and enjoy her time in childcare, as well as make good progress under the curriculum.

Children are naturally curious and should, in any childcare setting, have access to learning opportunities that allow them to discover how things work, the differences between shapes, textures, sounds and colours, and how simple problems can be solved. The more wide-ranging and diverse the opportunities on offer, the greater the scope for encouraging different personalities, aptitudes and preferred ways of learning amongst children of differing interests and abilities.

Other activities a good childcare provider will offer are role-play situations that allow children to learn about right and wrong as well as sharing, talking and listening, turn-taking and physical motor skills.

Above all, childcare must put the child's needs first. According to Professor Edward Melhuish from the Institute for the Study of Children, who in 2004 published a report into the importance of investing in quality childcare: 'Caregiving needs routines in order to fulfil its aims such as providing a balanced curriculum of activities. However, children's activities should take precedence over adult convenience. Movement from a rule-driven, clock-driven routine to a child-oriented responsive routine will engage children more in their daily experience.'

What the professionals say

'We believe that children who attend a pre-school or nursery are usually more confident and able to follow a routine, giving them a head start when they begin school. Our input is crucial in a child's formative years, as the practitioner impacts on children's learning as they develop and up to adulthood.'

Nicola Myers and Gina Welsh,
Manager and Deputy Manager, Willowtree
Neighbourhood Nursery, Lincoln

'In most cases, both home and structured pre-school learning is beneficial to children. The pre-school and home environments combine to provide a mixture of learning opportunities and experiences.'

Gemma Verner, Pre-school Leader,
Shoebury Children's Centre, Southend

'All children benefit from being in a safe, welcoming, stimulating environment, no matter where this is. Some children need to have an understanding of rules (when to wash hands, to sit when eating and so on), but this is no reflection on parenting skills and these children need pre-school as do the children who need to be there for parents working. A benefit can only be measured in a child's face – if they enjoy and learn, then their facial expressions and body language will show you.'

Dawn Williams, Manager, City View Pre-school
and Nursery, Canterbury, Kent

'One of the most rewarding aspects of the job is seeing the children engrossed in a new experience and sharing their wonder and excitement with you. One of the most frustrating is the great deal of paperwork that takes up time that could otherwise be spent with the children.'

Lisa Harvey, Pre-school Leader, Doddington Green Neighbourhood Nursery, Birmingham

'Every child is as important to me as the next. I never realised that I could love so many children individually, especially after having three of my own, but there is a bond with each little one who comes under my care. It's fantastically rewarding to watch them flourish and develop as they grow, and to know that I've had a hand in that development.'

Pamela Donaldson, childminder of five years' standing, Arbroath

'Having a houseful of children has always been my dream, and because I was only able to have one child myself, caring for others has filled the gap in a most fulfilling and rewarding way. One of the best parts of the job is that I can enjoy babyhood and toddlerhood again and again – and seeing the children from time to time after they've left my care and started school is fantastic.'

Lilian Bennett, childminder with 10 years' experience, Carlisle

Structured time

The goals that accompany both the Early Years Foundation Stage frameworks aren't designed to put children under any pressure: the idea is that most of the time they feel they're simply playing and having fun without feeling that any formal learning is taking place, and without the need to compare their progress with that of their peers. Each day should be structured to include scheduled activities as well as free play. Children should have the opportunity to play outdoors every day, when weather allows, and to spend time in different groups as well as working independently. This will encourage the development of a broad spectrum of skills – physical, mental, social and emotional – as well as making each child's day interesting, challenging and enjoyable.

A well-planned day

Your childcare provider should forward-plan activities at least a week ahead of time, and should be able to show you a typical day's timetable. Children need to be able to make their own choices about the activities they'd like to engage in, and the length of time that they spend on each. A well-balanced day could go something like this – although all the activities on offer should be available throughout the day rather than at fixed times:

8 a.m. Breakfast with playleader, key worker or childminder plus other children. (Ideally, the children will be seated around a table to encourage good table manners and eating habits as well as social interaction.)

9 a.m. Songs, rhymes and poems that involve the children and encourage them to join in.

10.15 a.m. Healthy snack time: a piece of fruit plus milk or water.

10.30 a.m. Exploring textures/collage.

11.30 a.m. Outdoor free play, with opportunities to explore, climb, role play and interact with other children.

12 noon Lunch (preferably cooked on the premises) followed by nap/rest time.

1.30 p.m. Dressing up and role play.

2.30 p.m. Writing practice: pencil control and basic letter formation.

3 p.m. Painting, gluing and sticking.

4.30 p.m. Tea (preferably prepared on the premises).

5 p.m. Quiet story time.

6 p.m. Home.

With thanks to BUPA/Teddies Nurseries

Other positive signs to look for

Once you have satisfied yourself that the premises are safe and stimulating, the curriculum is being properly adhered to, the equipment is up to date and challenging, and the hours on offer fit in with your own requirements, there are some other signs to look out for that could help to confirm your choice of childcare; all relate to childcare staff themselves. You should be encouraged if you notice staff:

- joining in enthusiastically with the children's different activities

- being sympathetic to a child who is upset in any way
- responding quickly to a crying baby
- showing real affection to the children
- getting the children's attention in a positive, friendly way
- encouraging parental involvement (although there may be rules in place about when and how this happens)
- really listening to individual children
- taking a child's idiosyncracies into account
- seeming to enjoy the work.

Why some pre-school care can be better than none

In 2004 a significant government research project was carried out to try to determine the impact of early years education on children. It focused specifically on intellectual and social development. The project, known as the Effective Provision of Pre-School Education (EPPE), investigated the effects of home background and pre-school education on over 3,000 children up to age seven. It concluded that:

- some pre-school experience, compared to none, enhances a child's development, and the positive effect on intellectual and social development remains during the early years of primary school.

- an earlier start (i.e. before age three) is related to better intellectual development at ages six and seven, and to improved independence, concentration and sociability when a child enters primary school and at age six. Conversely, though, the report does state that 'high levels of group care before the age of three (and particularly before the age of two) were associated with higher levels of anti-social behaviour at age three'.
- full-time attendance doesn't mean better outcomes for children than part-time.
- disadvantaged children in particular can benefit significantly from good-quality pre-school experiences, especially if the provider caters for a mixture of social backgrounds.

The EPPE project also found that:

- children's progress was enhanced in settings where the providers were warm and responsive to individual needs.
- children's progress was greater in settings where staff had higher qualifications.
- progress in reading and maths at age six was better in children whose pre-school experience included high-quality literacy, maths and science provision.

What children say about childcare

'I love seeing my friends at nursery, and I like it when my pictures get put on the board.'

Eddie, four, from Aberystwyth

'Susie is like another auntie to me. She gives me cuddles and makes me laugh.'

Leanne, three, from Tower Hamlets, London, talking about her childminder

'I can read my name!'

Owen, two and a half, from Newcastle, Tyne & Wear, who attends state nursery

'My best thing is going to the park with Lili.'

Jenna, three-and-a-half, from Somerset, talking about her au pair

'I like Claudia because she looks after me when my mummy and daddy aren't there.'

Andrea, four, from mid-Glamorgan, talking about her nanny

'I love my after-school club because I can do my homework with my friends.'

Albert, six, from Leatherhead, Surrey

'When I go to my grandma's house, I don't miss my mummy so much.'

Lydia, four, from Inverness

'My teacher reminds me of my Auntie Alice!'

Liam, three and a half, from Hereford, talking about his pre-school teacher

Ten skills nurtured by quality childcare

Well-researched, paid-for childcare – whether it's a childminder, nanny, nursery, out-of-school provision, pre-school, playgroup, or friends and family – should provide your child with some early education. Under the Childcare Act 2006 (see page 33), two new frameworks for learning and development for children up to age five have been implemented. As discussed earlier, these frameworks are known jointly as the Early Years Foundation Stage, and they bring together the existing 'Birth to Three Matters' and 'Foundation Stage' frameworks as well as national standards for daycare and childminding. In other words, all paid providers looking after under-fives will be expected to deliver the Early Years Foundation Stage; they'll also have to be registered and they'll be inspected regularly by Ofsted. Other unpaid care providers, such as friends and family, can become registered voluntarily if they wish to.

The key skills that any form of childcare should nurture in your child include:

- sociability
- self-expression
- the ability to share
- communication skills
- advanced language development
- turn-taking
- teamwork
- confidence
- early letter and shape formation
- early number comprehension.

What the government is doing

Under the government's Sure Start programme, which was set up in the 1990s to support children and help parents to balance work and family commitments, early years care and family services – particularly in deprived areas – are undergoing improvement and are monitored closely. Sure Start Children's Centres, offering services including healthcare for children, advice on parenting, pre-natal classes, and information about jobs, training, housing, healthy eating and work, have been set up throughout the UK. The aim is that there will be a Children's Centre for every UK community by 2010.

So far the government has provided, through the Centres, over 617,000 new registered childcare places. There's also now guaranteed, free early education on offer for all three- and four-year-olds; the Working Tax Credit has been introduced to help with childcare costs and the Childcare Act 2006 has been implemented to build on Sure Start's progress.

Free early years education for all

On 1 April 2006, all three- and four-year-olds became entitled to free early years education, funded by the government, for up to 12.5 hours per week, 38 weeks of the year. This provision is available to children for six terms from the start of the term following their third birthday, and is explained in more detail on page 52. The places are available in settings that have been inspected by Ofsted and found to be satisfactory in terms of quality, including private, voluntary and independent groups, as well as registered childminder networks. Parents may be charged fees for any services or childcare over and above this entitlement.

What the Childcare Act 2006 means

According to the government, the Childcare Act of 2006 'guarantees accessible, high-quality childcare and other services for children under five, and gives parents greater choice in balancing work and family'.

Responsibility for childcare provision now lies with local authorities, who are responsible for raising the standards and accessibility of childcare, and getting measurably better results. For details of the care available to you, contact your local education authority or visit www.direct.gov.uk.

Under the Act:

- all children under five will have access to high-quality early learning and care, and better access to free care and learning where required. This provision will increase and become more flexible for those parents of three- and four-year-olds who want it.
- nursery education provision in schools, pre-schools, day nurseries and with accredited childminders is regularly inspected by Ofsted (www.ofsted.gov.uk) and is supported by a team of Early Years advisers who ensure high-quality care and education.

- the Early Years Foundation Stage – a high-quality learning and development framework for children from birth to age five – will be adhered to by all childcare providers on the Early Years register.
- working parents will be offered a wide choice of childcare.
- reforms will be made to the regulation of childcare providers in order to provide parents with greater confidence about the childcare they choose.
- local authorities are to provide better 'joined up' and accessible early childhood services in the most deprived areas of the country through Children's Centres, at least one of which will feature in every community by 2010 under the government's 10-year childcare strategy. The centres are open for a minimum of 10 hours a day, five days a week, 48 weeks a year.

Add to all this the government's plan that by 2015 at least 60% of staff working in pre-school nurseries should be educated to graduate level, and the picture is looking more reassuring than ever before.

Positive effects of childcare on parents

Many parents' relationships with their children flourish as a result of spending a little regular time apart. Here are some of the things parents have said:

'Once we knew that Robert was happy with our childminder, Helen, and he'd adapted to his routine

of two afternoons a week with her, I felt more in control as a parent. Beforehand, I'd find myself getting to the end of my tether with Robert just because he was such a demanding baby – I used to cry my way through the day sometimes. Now supermarket shopping is something I actually look forward to doing on my own! Helen's calming influence has also had a knock-on effect and Robert is more contented generally.'

Lesley, 32, mum to Robert, six months

'I had no idea how full on parenting would be before I had Grace. I struggled on for over a year feeling that I was an inadequate wife as well as mum because I couldn't even find time to sort the washing out most days. Then a neighbour told me her son was attending a nearby private nursery, and I went to visit. Grace started there, mornings only, when she was about 14 months old and we haven't looked back. Despite the financial hardship, just being able to straighten the house out and prepare a meal ahead of time has made me a much happier person, and that makes me a better mum, too.'

Sheila, 25, mum to Grace, 18 months

'I thought I'd never want to go back to work and was amazed to realise how much I missed adult company after just two months of motherhood. It wasn't practical to go back to my old job because of the travelling costs and journey time, but my mum-in-law suggested I find local work, and offered to do some childcare. I now work as a part-time doctors' receptionist and I love it. It's only two days a week,

but that adult contact means such a lot and makes me appreciate Kyle more. He is doing brilliantly well and enjoying spending more time with his granny.'

Surinda, 24, mum to Kyle, five months

'People have said that being a working mum is a lifestyle choice, and that if we moved to a smaller house, I'd be able to give up work: that used to make me feel terrible. But the fact is we're planning to have at least two more children, so we'll need all the space we can get – and I need to work in order to save up for a larger family. Charlotte goes to a pre-school playgroup four mornings a week during school term times and I work from home, so I think that's a fair compromise. She's much more sociable than ever before, and we're not struggling to make ends meet. Also, I don't feel guilty if I spend a bit of money on myself as I'm still contributing to the family finances.'

Gill, 31, mum to Charlotte, three

Better provision for working parents

Under the government's 'Ten Year Strategy for Childcare', it will be up to schools to offer 'wraparound' childcare. This means that schools will open earlier, perhaps having breakfast clubs where the children will be offered a wholesome and nutritious meal, and they will close later, so that parents have more flexibility for negotiating their working hours. The aim is that by 2010 all children aged five to 11 will have access to affordable, school-based childcare all year round, and all secondary schools will be open from 8 a.m. to 6 p.m. during the week.

This scheme, too, has its critics, with the main concern being that children will be spending too much time in school and not enough at home with their parents. But for many families it will mean greater potential for both parents to work.

> *'The idea of Ayesha being at school for as long as most workers are away from home doesn't appeal to me on a full-time basis, but if it means I can work two full days a week rather than the four nights I currently have to do, it will be less stressful all round. I'm sure her school will have fun clubs and stuff for her to do that she'll really enjoy – and we'll still have three afternoons together out of five when I won't be rushing around getting dinner and preparing to go off to work.'*
>
> Letitia, 29, mum to Ayesha, seven

Why consistency of care is key

In a long-term study of children from birth to the age of six years, carried out by the Institute for the Study of Children, it was found that where childcare arrangements were erratic or otherwise unstable during the first three years of life, language development suffered, and this remained the case until age six. Further studies showed also that young children formed stronger attachments to well-known carers than to less familiar people, and that instability of care resulted in more aggressive behaviour amongst these children than in those who had formed strong attachments.

Chapter 3

What you can expect from paid childcare

Now that you have read about the benefits of childcare to you and your child, and are familiar with the qualities that make positive childcare provision a good thing, you need to discover what's on offer from different providers. This chapter covers paid childcare, including unregistered, unregulated forms of care such as that offered by nannies and au pairs. You could be entitled to help with paying for certain types of childcare under the Working Tax Credit and Childcare Voucher schemes (see page 169 for details).

Registered childcare

Day nursery

Day nurseries offer full-time, all-year-round daycare for children aged between six weeks and five years (although some won't take babies younger than three months), with some offering out-of-school provision for five- to 11-year-olds (see page 107). Some nurseries open from as early as 7 a.m. and close as late as 7 p.m.; others open from 8 a.m. to 6 p.m. daily. They may be privately run or they may be community, council or workplace nurseries, with costs depending on subsidies and families' personal circumstances.

Most nurseries offer breakfast, lunch and tea, with vegetarian options and concessions to food allergies and other special dietary requirements. Healthy snacks and drinks should be given in between. Day nurseries often have a minimum requirement for frequency of attendance – for example, at least two half-day sessions per week.

All day nurseries are subject to an annual inspection by Ofsted, but some have additional accreditation through the National Day Nurseries Association (NDNA). The Quality Counts (QC) kite-mark is an indicator to parents of an independent assessment of quality that is deemed to be over and above the National Standard (see page 56). You can search the NDNA's database for a list of accredited nurseries in your area by visiting www.ndna.org.uk.

At least half the staff in a day nursery must have an Early Years qualification, and there must be some staff with teaching qualifications, too. Nurseries are expected to follow the government's Early Years Foundation Stage curriculum.

Private nurseries are independently run businesses that may either be one-off enterprises or have other branches or franchises.

Community nurseries operate on a not-for-profit basis, so the fees are generally lower than those of private nurseries. Some apply a sliding scale of costs, depending on each individual family's financial situation.

Workplace nurseries are operated by employers, and places are usually available only to their employees – except, in some cases, where places remain unfilled after all employees' needs have been catered for.

Local authority nurseries exist mainly for families who are on income support. They usually open during playgroup/ school hours, from around 9 a.m. to 3 p.m., and may offer free places to under-privileged children.

Some criteria will differ from nursery to nursery; others must be consistent throughout all nurseries. Some nurseries will only accept children who are below school-age, whilst others will accept children up to age eight for out-of-school care: this is a decision that's down to the individual nurseries.

In the case of adult-to-child ratios, though, there is a legal requirement for one adult for every three children under the age of two, or one adult for every two babies if there is a high intake of babies (extra staff should be taken on in this eventuality); one adult for every four two-year-olds; one adult for every eight children aged between three and eight years. (Places are sometimes available to children from five to eight years old as before- and/or after-school care.)

Pros

- Nurseries must be registered by law and are subject to annual Ofsted inspections.
- Opening hours fit in well around most parents' working day.
- Open all year round.
- Good levels of experienced and qualified staff.
- Structured learning in line with the government's Early Years Foundation Stage.
- Good for the general socialisation of children, as well as teaching skills such as sharing, turn-taking and teamwork.
- If one staff member is sick, cover can be found.
- If one child is proving difficult, key workers may swap children temporarily to support each other.
- Staff can monitor and observe each other.

Cons

- Although your child will be assigned a 'key worker' who will report to you on a day-to-day basis on his progress, a team of people is responsible for your child, so he will have to get used to and forge relationships with several different adults within a short space of time.
- Your child will be away from his own home.
- If you're using a private nursery, the fees can be high. (Depending on your family income, you may be eligible for some help with fees – see page 169.)

Once your child reaches three or four, he might be offered a free place as part of the government's pledge.)

- Unless you put your child's name down in advance of his birth, you may have to wait for a place to become available. This is often true of the most popular nurseries, so do make enquiries as soon as you possibly can.
- If your child has a notifiable illness, he won't be able to attend nursery until he has been clear of symptoms for a specified time. This is usually the case if he contracts headlice, too.
- If your child falls ill during the working day, you will be expected to collect him (or arrange for a nominated person who can be identified by the nursery to collect him) as soon as possible after you are called.
- If there is a high staff turnover, your child may bond with his key worker or other staff member only to lose them soon after and have to form new bonds. (This can be particularly tricky with a shy, slow-to-warm-up child.)
- There is little flexibility around pick-up times – usually because adult-to-child ratios fall outside legal limits as staff leave to go home – and you may be charged for lateness.

What it will cost

The cost of a private nursery place varies enormously depending on where in the UK you live, as well as other factors. Expect to pay anything between £75 and £250 per week for a full-time place. This works out to between £7.50 and £25 per morning or afternoon session. Fees generally tend to reduce as the adult-to-child ratio requirement diminishes, so you will pay less as your child gets older. Local authority nurseries may be free or you may have to pay a nominal amount for your child's midday meal, but you will usually have to be referred to get a free place.

Pre-school or playgroup

Pre-schools and playgroups have always provided care and play opportunities for three- to five-year-olds, but most are now on board with providing early education, too, and all attendees should be enjoying activities laid down in the Early Years Foundation Stage frameworks. In England and Wales, many primary schools operate an early admission policy where they admit children under five years old into reception classes.

Pre-schools and playgroups are run by the local community on a not-for-profit basis, and volunteer parent helpers often make up the required adult-to-child ratios, which are the same as for nurseries (see page 41). Morning or afternoon sessions last between two and a half and four hours. Some groups offer morning and afternoon sessions every week day; others have more restricted hours or days available. All groups operate during school term times only, although some are restructuring to offer more flexible sessions or even full-time, year-round daycare. Waiting lists, as for nurseries, can be long, so it's worth making enquiries and visits well in advance of when you may need a place.

Pros

- Registered pre-schools and playgroups are regularly inspected by Ofsted.
- The informal environment means most children are relaxed and ready to socialise.
- Most staff are trained in formal childcare or are in the midst of training – and in pre-schools the leader must have a level 3 qualification plus trained staff.
- Playgroups and pre-school groups can be useful as supplementary childcare if you are using an au pair, nanny, childminder, friend or relative.
- Pre-schools and playgroups are relatively inexpensive (although charges will vary depending on where in the UK you live).
- Whilst groups are increasingly focused on early years education as well as play, the main emphasis is still on learning through play.
- Groups are usually situated centrally rather than out of town.

Cons

- Limited hours and session times mean that these groups are really only an option for part-time local workers, parents who stay at home or those who can rely on someone else to collect and care for their children out of session times.
- It is down to the individual groups whether or not they offer early education or whether the sessions are simply play times.

- Because they are run on a not-for-profit basis, facilities and equipment may be limited or in need of refurbishment.
- Groups can be large and tend to congregate in one room: most will take between 24 and 28 children per session.

What it will cost

The costs are minimal at around £3–£5 per session but with regional variations. Fees may be payable weekly, but are more usually asked for by the term or half-term. Visit www.childcarelink.org.uk for details of groups near you and their charges.

Childminder

Childminders provide childcare in their own homes for children from newborn to teenage, and are able to care for up to six children under the age of eight, including their own, at a time. Out of the six, however, only three children can be under the age of five. Childminders are self-employed, so they set their own hours and charges, and they have a final say in what's included.

Some childminders are happy to work out of normal hours – for example, early mornings, some evenings or even part weekends: it's up to you to negotiate your terms. It's usual for childminders to expect payment during holidays and when your child is sick, although you won't usually have to pay if they are sick themselves.

All minders must, by law, be registered by Ofsted; all must have completed training that includes a module on providing quality play activities across the age range as well as basic first aid. Many do go on to gain further qualifications, and all are now expected to provide learning opportunities suitable for your child's age and developmental stage, to coincide with the government's Early Years Foundation Stage frameworks. They are subject to regular Ofsted inspections when both the childminder and her home are assessed. Childminders must also have public liability insurance, and must have undergone a health check and an enhanced Criminal Records Bureau (CRB) disclosure. Anyone else aged 16 or over who lives or works in the childminder's home must also have been CRB checked.

Pros

- Your child will be cared for in a home environment.
- He will forge a relationship with his childminder, who will have exclusive care of him during daycare hours.
- He will be mixing with a limited number of other children, some of whom will be his age.
- Your child will benefit from one-to-one care.
- You will be able to negotiate hours and terms to suit you.
- Childminders are often prepared to be flexible about the occasional late pick-up if you are delayed at work.
- Many parents form lasting friendships with their children's minders.

- Your child's day may be less structured than in a more formal childcare setting (although some parents may consider this to be a negative thing).

Cons

- If your childminder is having a difficult period with your child (or another under her care), she has no one else to take over temporarily. This can be stressful for both minder and child.
- You must pay her holiday pay.
- You'll need to have a contingency carer in place for times when your childminder or one of her own children is sick, and for when she takes holiday.
- Your child's day may be less structured than in a more formal childcare setting (although some parents may regard this as positive).
- Your minder may have less access to technology and play equipment than other childcare providers.

What it will cost

Costs vary enormously from area to area and between individual minders. The national average for full-time care for a child under the age of two is around £130 per week, but you may pay up to £350 per week in London and the southeast where some minders charge £7 per hour.

Sure Start Children's Centre

More than simply childcare providers, Sure Start Children's Centres offer a range of care and services to families – especially the under-privileged – and children from pregnancy to age five. You can approach your local Sure

Start Centre for advice on finding a job yourself, finding a childminder, accessing education about parenting, seeking support and much more. The government's pledge is to provide 3,500 Children's Centres by 2010.

Not all staff are employed directly by the centre, and different centres have different staffing structures depending on local demand and where the emphasis for the various services lies. As a guideline, each centre's staff is likely to include:

- a manager.
- qualified teachers who will lead early learning activities in line with the government's Early Years Foundation Stage frameworks.
- nursery assistants or nursery nurses, who will be closely involved in the children's welfare and development.
- family support staff who can intervene between families and social services as well as other service providers.
- health professionals (such as health visitors and speech and language therapists).
- childminders and a childminder network coordinator.
- Jobcentre Plus staff.

Pros

- If you are financially disadvantaged or on state benefits, you may be eligible for free childcare at these centres.

- The centres are a one-stop shop for other information and advice.
- They are open for a minimum 48 weeks a year, five days a week, 10 hours a day.
- Early education is on offer for all children from birth to five.
- They provide an opportunity to meet other locally based families.

Cons

- Because of their one-stop nature, the centres are less personal than smaller, more intimate childcare settings.
- The care is provided by a team of staff, so your child will have to form relationships with several adults and other children at once.
- Some families have allegedly found the centres intimidating and unapproachable – and these have included the most needy, at whom they are primarily aimed. However, the government is taking steps to address this problem.

What it will cost

Each centre will be run according to the needs of the population it serves, so your best bet is to contact your local centre direct. You may be expected to pay for childcare, depending on your personal and financial circumstances.

Nursery school or class

Nursery schools can be state run, community run or private and are independent of primary schools. Each has its own staff of trained teachers, including headteacher, nursery nurses and classroom assistants. Nursery classes, on the other hand, are attached to primary schools, both state run and private, and share their staff and headteachers with the main schools.

Both nursery schools and classes offer early education and childcare for children aged two and a half (or, in some case, three) to five years. The fees will vary from region to region in community-run and private provision, although your child may be entitled to a free place.

Nursery schools/classes offer children daily morning or afternoon sessions during school term time. You will usually be allocated mornings or afternoons rather than a mix of both, and some providers also offer all-day places. All schools, both state and private, are being encouraged to provide extended hours to include full daycare, and some are already offering out-of-school care and holiday cover (see page 54).

Nursery schools/classes follow the government's Early Years Foundation Stage frameworks for education, so your child should experience learning opportunities appropriate to his age and developmental stage. Most nursery leaders generally prefer children to be able to make themselves understood and to be fully toilet-trained before joining – although, because of the early age of entry, many will make allowances.

Age of eligibility for free childcare

This table shows when your child will become eligible for a free early education childcare place.

If your child is born between:	They are eligible for a free place from:
1 April and 31 August	1 September following their third birthday until statutory school age
1 September and 31 December	1 January following their third birthday until statutory school age
1 January and 31 March	1 April following their third birthday until statutory school age

Pros

- All nursery schools and classes have to be registered and are subject to regular Ofsted inspections.
- Your child will be taught in line with the Early Years Foundation Stage frameworks by a qualified teacher.
- The experience of being in a classroom gives children a good taste of what's to come when they start school – and this is further enhanced where the nursery school is attached to the primary school that it feeds into.
- Children learn some of the disciplines they'll encounter at school.
- Your child may meet and mix with children who will eventually join the primary school with him.

- Your child will mix only with similar-age children.
- There will always be someone on hand to look after your child, even if the nursery teacher is sick.
- Where full daycare is offered, it can fit in well with your working day.

Cons

- Staff-to-child ratios are less stringent than in nurseries and pre-school playgroups, with only one adult allocated to every 10–13 children.
- If full daycare is not on offer, morning- or afternoon-only sessions mean that, as with pre-school playgroups, this type of care is suitable only for local part-time workers, stay-at-home parents or those who can rely on someone else to collect their child and care for him for the rest of the day.
- Some children find the discipline of school nurseries difficult to cope with at such a young age.
- Your child will effectively be 'institutionalised' from an early age until he leaves school.
- Not all three-year-olds are reliably toilet-trained and/or can communicate their needs effectively (although many nursery schools and/or classes will make allowances in the cases of younger children).

What it will cost

It's free if it's part of a state education system, but expect to pay around £3.50 per session for a community nursery place and between £800 and £1,200 per term for full-time private provision.

Out-of-school care

Out-of-school care can come in several different guises, but basically constitutes care offered outside of school hours for two or more hours per day. It's available only for children who have started full-time school. You may find care is offered as breakfast clubs, homework clubs, after-school clubs, holiday play schemes or summer camps. Childminders may also offer out-of-hours care (see page 46). Clubs are usually run in schools, but may also be organised in youth clubs, local libraries, nurseries or community centres. Each local authority will hold details of the provision on offer in that particular area of the UK.

The government is planning that by 2010 all schools will provide all-year-round 'extended services' (also known as 'wraparound' or out-of-hours childcare) from 8 a.m. until 6 p.m. on weekdays. The Working Tax Credit is available for some types of out-of-hours care.

There are national standards laid down for out-of-school care provision, and all bodies offering out-of-school care for children up to the age of eight, whether they are schools or other centres, must be registered and regularly inspected by Ofsted. Playworkers must be trained or qualified, as must at least half of all staff.

Pros

- Out-of-school care offers more scope for working parents to negotiate their hours to fit in with childcare.
- It's relatively inexpensive (see page 55).

- Your child is likely to be mixing with established friends and has the opportunity to form new friendships.
- Out-of-school care offers holiday cover – a major stumbling block for most working parents.
- It's consistent.
- It gives your child an opportunity to eat a healthy breakfast.
- Your child may have completed his homework before he comes home.

Cons

- Children are away from home for as long as their working parents.
- Your child may be getting his homework support from someone other than you.
- You will probably have less involvement in your child's day and homework.

What it will cost

Costs vary from provider to provider, but for state provision expect to pay, on average, between £5 and £11 per day for an after-school club, and around £15 per day (£75 per week) for a holiday place. Privately run clubs and play schemes cost around double that amount: on average, £150 per week. Charges for breakfast clubs vary: some are funded by health authorities or local business, so placements are free; others charge around £2–£4 per session.

Montessori nurseries

Some parents regard Montessori nurseries more as structured learning centres than as daycare, but Montessori still comes under the banner of pre-school care, so I include here a section on this option.

Dr Maria Montessori's approach to education was to identify each child's individual needs. She believed that teachers properly trained in her methods could make children confident self-educators, equipped and prepared for the future. The Montessori approach is based on educating the whole child in all aspects of development, including intellectual, social, physical, emotional and spiritual. The emphasis is on self-reliance, and there is little formal testing of children.

Children attending Montessori nurseries are routinely given opportunities to develop important life skills, and are taught to dress and undress themselves, practising with buttons, zips and bows. They also look after the classroom, using little brushes and dusters to keep things spick and span. Children are schooled in mixed age groups according to ability, and also coached in practical skills, such as pouring drinks and laying the table. In addition, there is a focus on social skills with friends and teachers, and great emphasis on the importance of family life.

What it will cost

Montessori nursery fees and session times vary widely from place to place so, although it's fair to say that there will be considerable fees involved in securing a place, it's best to contact individual nurseries for details of their rates.

National Standards for daycare and childminding

The government has laid down National Standards with which all registered childcarers (i.e. providers caring for children up to age eight) must comply. These come under 14 categories, and are described as follows:

Standard 1: Suitable person
Adults providing daycare, looking after children or having unsupervised access to them are suitable to do so.

Standard 2: Organisation
The registered person meets required adult-to-child ratios, ensures that training and qualifications requirements are met and organises space and resources to meet the children's needs effectively.

Standard 3: Care, learning and play
The registered person meets children's individual needs and promotes their welfare. They plan and provide activities and play opportunities to develop children's emotional, physical, social and intellectual capabilities.

Standard 4: Physical environment
The premises are safe, secure and suitable for their purpose. They provide adequate space in an appropriate location, are welcoming to children and offer access to the necessary facilities for a range of activities that promote their development.

Standard 5: Equipment
Furniture, equipment and toys are provided that are appropriate for their purpose and help to create an accessible and stimulating environment. They are of suitable design and condition, well maintained and conform to safety standards.

Standard 6: Safety
The registered person takes positive steps to promote safety within the setting and on outings and ensures proper precautions are taken to prevent accidents.

Standard 7: Health
The registered person promotes the good health of children and takes positive steps to prevent the spread of infection, and appropriate measures when they are ill.

Standard 8: Food and drink
Children are provided with regular drinks and food in adequate quantities for their needs. Food and drink is properly prepared, nutritious and complies with dietary and religious requirements.

Standard 9: Equal opportunities
The registered person and staff actively promote equality of opportunity and anti-discriminatory practice for all children.

Standard 10: Special needs (including special educational needs and disabilities)
The registered person is aware that some children may have special needs and is proactive in ensuring that

appropriate action can be taken when such a child is identified or admitted to the provision. Steps are taken to promote the welfare and development of the child within the setting, in partnership with the parents and other relevant parties.

Standard 11: Behaviour
Adults caring for children in the provision are able to manage a wide range of children's behaviour in a way that promotes their welfare and development.

Standard 12: Working in partnerships with parents and carers
The registered person and staff work in partnership with parents to meet the needs of the children, both individually and as a group. Information is shared.

Standard 13: Child protection
The registered person complies with the local child protection procedure approved by the Area Child Protection Committee and ensures that all adults working and looking after children in the provision are able to put the procedures into practice.

Standard 14: Documentation
Records, policies and procedures that are required for the efficient and safe management of the provision, and to promote the welfare, care and learning of children, are maintained. Records about individual children are shared with the child's parent.

Unregistered childcare

Nanny

There are two essential differences between nannies and childminders. First, nannies usually work for one family at a time (although some families work out a 'nanny share' arrangement). Second, they tend to live and work in the home of the child they are caring for, rather than in their own homes, although a small proportion do live out. You will not be eligible for financial help with childcare if you hire a nanny.

Nannies should be either qualified childcare professionals, or have had at least two years' experience of childcare. A widely recognised qualification to look for is the DCE (Diploma in Childcare and Education) awarded by CACHE (Council for Awards in Childcare and Education), formerly known as the NNEB or the DNN. Otherwise, look for a BTEC National Diploma in Childhood Studies or NVQ (National Vocational Qualification) level 3.

Nannies tend to work a five-day week, whether living in or out. Surveys indicate that many nannies work 50–60 hours per week, but it's worth knowing that they are covered by the government's Working Time Directive, which limits a working week to 48 hours. Generally speaking, most live-out nannies will expect to work up to 10 hours a day at the outside and be paid extra for babysitting. A live-in nanny's wages are usually calculated to include one or two nights' babysitting per week. Unlike au pairs, nannies are not expected to undertake housework of any kind, although your nanny should be prepared to clear up after herself and your child.

Most nannies live in the family home with their own rooms, but a few prefer to live independently and come to work each day. Unlike other more formal childcare provision, nannies don't have to be registered, are not limited by the number of children they can care for and are not subject to inspection or Criminal Records Bureau checks. You can't request a CRB check on a potential nanny yourself, but if she comes via an agency, the agent can instigate one, so it's worth finding out which agencies do this as a matter of course. There is a new government initiative whereby nannies can become 'approved' under the Childcare Approval Scheme, and you may want to restrict interviews to individuals who have taken this step. For more information about this scheme, visit www.childcareapprovalscheme.co.uk.

Pros

- Your child will be cared for in his own home, surrounded by his own toys, books and familiar things.
- If your nanny lives in, there's more scope for flexible hours or spontaneous extra hours in return for other perks or more pay.
- Siblings can be looked after together.
- Your child will have just the one carer to form a bond with.
- Care is one-to-one.
- You can control your child's environment, diet and activities better when the care is in your own home.
- Your nanny may be willing to babysit for extra money.

- Your nanny can take your child to his usual clubs and activities.
- Your nanny will usually still care for your child if he falls ill.
- You may be able to negotiate a 'nanny share' whereby your nanny splits her time (and her charges) between two or more families.

Cons

- The costs are higher than for any other kind of childcare.
- You will have to pay your nanny's tax and National Insurance and generate a payslip (see page 172).
- When your nanny leaves your employment, it can be a wrench for your child if he has forged a strong bond.
- Not all families enjoy having an outsider in their homes – especially living in.
- It's down to you to vet your prospective nanny, as they are not subject to inspection, registration or CRB checks.
- Nannies do not have to follow any specific early years education programme and are not expected to adhere to the government's Early Years Foundation Stage curriculum.

What it will cost

Costs vary, but the national average for a live-in nanny to earn is £230–£300 net per week, plus food and board. Live-out nannies tend to earn £300–£450 per week rising, whereas part-time or temporary nanny care is typically charged out at £7–£9 per hour.

Au pair
The Recruitment and Employment Confederation (REC) stipulates that au pairs should never have sole charge of children under the age of three, so this option is not for you if your child has not yet had his third birthday. An au pair will care for your child in your own home for a modest wage (see page 65) plus free board and lodging, including a room of her own. She (or he) will be a young adult aged 17–27 who has come to England in order to learn the language. In most cases au pairs have a college course to follow; sometimes their English is very limited when they arrive. They don't need to have any experience or training in caring for children and are not eligible to offer full-time childcare. You will not be able to claim financial help with childcare if you hire an au pair.

According to Home Office rules, au pairs can work up to a maximum 25 hours per week with two days off. Most au pairs will offer an additional two evenings babysitting per week. (Some agencies offer 'au pairs plus', who will work up to 35 hours per week and should be paid accordingly. However, this arrangement is questionable and does not fall strictly in line with Home Office rules.)

Au pairs tend to stay with the same family for six months and this usually means that, as employer, you need not offer a paid holiday as they are deemed to have worked only part time. However, if the au pair stays for longer than six months, there's a case for agreeing to a period of paid, and perhaps some unpaid, holiday.

Pros

- Your child is more likely to build a strong bond with a carer who lives in the family home.
- He may bond more readily with a younger person.
- It's relatively inexpensive to hire an au pair (see page 65).
- Hours can be more flexible than with other arrangements.
- Babysitting is free for two nights a week, as long as you agree this up front.
- Light housework may be included in your agreement, as long as it falls within the au pair's five hours' work per day.

Cons

- Au pairs are usually unqualified and often without childcare experience.
- The language barrier may make life difficult at first.
- Standards of housework can vary enormously!
- You will have to train your au pair in childcare and first aid.
- You'll need to organise back-up care in case of an emergency.
- It can be difficult to share your home with a stranger – especially when communication is difficult.
- You are limited by the five-hour daily working time restriction.

- You will have to insure your au pair to drive your car.
- Your child may be upset when the au pair eventually leaves.
- Your au pair will probably want to use your phone/ car during some of her/his free time.

What it will cost

Free board and lodging and pocket money of roughly £60 to £75 per week, to be negotiated between you and the agency or the au pair direct, plus phone and car costs (all to be negotiated between you). Your utility bills are likely to increase because of the extra use during the daytime.

STOP PRESS!

From 2008 all registered childcarers must, under controversial, brand-new legislation, monitor children's progress from to birth to age five towards 69 different early learning goals. These include assessing the different ways babies communicate, such as babbling and gurgling, and scrutinising the skills they will need to start writing and number work. There is concern amongst early-years groups that adult-to-child staff ratios will make the effective monitoring of every child impossible, but it remains to be seen, when the legislation comes into practice, how these difficulties may be overcome.

Chapter 4

Using family as childminders

The majority of families choose to use their own relatives (or friends) to some degree as childcare providers, either full or part time, or as part of a broader arrangement. Some parents, for instance, mix grandparent care with a nursery place, pre-school or childminder. Whatever proportion of care your relative or friend offers, it's an arrangement that can work very well in terms of flexibility, affordability and the fact that your child is being looked after by someone who knows and loves her, and who has her best interests at heart.

One of the beauties of having a relative or friend as carer is that there is an established bond of trust, and you all know each other and your child intimately. If your child is to be cared for in your own home, your relative or friend will probably know their way around it and will feel comfortable operating within it. If they are caring for your child in their own home, this will also be familiar territory to your child, who will probably come to see it as a second home, and perhaps be able to leave some of her own toys, books, CDs and DVDs there permanently.

It's natural to think that there can be no better arrangement than to have someone who is close to you and your child caring for her, but there are downsides, too: some studies have shown that unregistered, home-based care like this can hold children back educationally – probably because registered carers now have a responsibility to follow the government's Early Years Foundation Stage curriculum as part of their care. It's easy, too, to take a relative or friend for granted, or to expect them to know, without prior discussion, exactly how to react to your child in all situations and what you will or won't approve of in terms of discipline and rewards. Then there is the possibility of a conflict of opinion based on experience, and this is most likely to occur between you and your parent, in-law or other relative who already has children.

Granny knows best?

While I am concentrating on grandparents here, the same advice applies for a friend of the family or any other relative. Grandparents in particular – who have raised children of their own and are always likely to regard themselves as having a greater accumulation of valuable life experience than you – may find it difficult to see eye to eye with you on all aspects of childcare. Discipline can be an issue, with grandparents being either too indulgent or too strict. Routines can break down if not adhered to by all your child's carers, and this disruption can result in insecurity in your child as well as conflict in her relationship with her carer. All of this can put a strain on your relationship with your parent or in-law – and it can be hard for either side to voice a complaint in case of hurt feelings, awkwardness or a loss of willingness on the part of the carer to continue with the arrangement.

> *'When my mum-in-law, whom I adore, offered to care for Mae-Lin for us, I was over the moon and thought all my troubles were at an end. It's been a real struggle, however, to get her to appreciate that continuity is important in a toddler's life. Almost every other day, Mae-Lin misses out on her afternoon nap because they've been out shopping or feeding the ducks instead. Then she comes home so overtired that I can't get her to sleep at bedtime. My mum-in-law also gives her too many sweets, and then I have trouble every time I get to a supermarket checkout because Mae-Lin will go into a tantrum when she sees the sweets and I won't buy them for her. In some ways, it would have been easier to pay someone to care for Mae-Lin. I wouldn't have such an issue with someone who's formally employed.'*
>
> Amy Chang, 33, mum to Mae-Lin, two

Establishing ground rules

The fact remains that, whether or not any money changes hands (and we will come to remuneration later on), you are still 'employing' your relative to take care of your child and, as such, you have both entered into a contract. There needs to be some sort of agreement drawn up between you before the arrangement begins, so it's best to make it clear right from the outset that you believe things will work out only if a set of mutually agreed rules is established. You might want to allow for a few concessions to be made – after all, your mum, for instance, might have some of ideas of her own that she'd like to incorporate into your child's day, and this is fair enough, especially given that she is a perfectly competent parent in her own right: just agree that these will slot in amongst the child's normal routine. As long as your child realises that any special treats or privileges are specific to Granny's house, and not to be expected at home, things should work out fine.

Drawing up an informal contract

Start by drawing up an informal list of your preferred dos and don'ts. As discussed above, it's a good idea from the point of view of diplomacy to chat these through with your relative rather than presenting a list of rules and regulations that are 'written in stone'. Areas you might want to open up for discussion, which are explored in more detail in the pages following, include:

- diet
- discipline
- nap times
- treats and privileges
- TV time
- toilet habits
- comforters.

Diet

If you have firm ideas about what you are and aren't happy for your child to eat and drink, make this clear from the start. It doesn't matter whether it's a case of personal preference or whether your child has an allergy or sensitivity to certain things: as long as you are specific about her requirements, there shouldn't be any problem with your relative or friend going along with your wishes. If your child does have an allergy, it's even more important that you give clear, explicit instructions; you may even prefer providing her own foods for her carer to serve to her.

It can be really hard to reason with parents or in-laws if they don't agree with your thinking. You might, for example, hear: 'What's wrong with a chocolate biscuit every now and then? She's only going to want one when she sees me having mine anyway.' You could respond by saying, for example: 'I'd prefer you not to give her a chocolate biscuit, even if you're having one, because she must learn that rules for adults are different.' For more suggestions to help you make your point without giving offence, see page 82.

Discipline

Do stand firm on this, as mixed methods of discipline will only confuse your child, resulting in erratic behaviour. Make it clear how you discipline her at home, with an explanation of the thinking behind your method. If you use 'time out', for example, describe how you arrive at the amount of time your child spends alone (typically one minute for each year of her life) and how you react if she decides to defy you. You should be as specific as possible, even down to the tone of voice you use when disciplining. If your child sees you and her carer forming a united front, she's far less likely to try to break the rules away from home – and you might find that her behaviour at home improves, too, as a result of this affirmation.

Be very clear about corporal punishment: if your parent or in-law is in favour of smacking, take a firm stance and make it clear that this is simply not acceptable. Point out that the law now allows for a prison sentence of up to five years for anyone found to have marked a child through corporal punishment, and even though 'mild smacking' (however that is interpreted) is still legal, many groups, including the child protection charity National Society for the Prevention of Cruelty to Children (NSPCC), believe it should be banned once and for all.

Nap times

It's not necessarily easy for someone else – however close they are to your child – to put her down for a nap. She's used to your voice, smell and general presence to help her get off to sleep, and may very well rail against someone else trying to take over. The key is for her carer to establish a regular routine, right from day one. It will probably take them both a week or so to settle into it, but perseverance should pay off sooner rather than later. You might find that a slight variance from your home routine will work better with Granny, so that comparisons with her home routine aren't automatically drawn: perhaps Granny has an old teddy or favourite storybook to share with your child? Maybe she'll drink some warm milk for Granny, but not for you. It doesn't matter if things are done differently, as long it's clear that what happens at Granny's is special to her house and what happens at home will stay the same as usual (unless, of course, Granny's method works better in both homes or vice versa!). Do make sure, though, that conditions don't change too much: if, for example, you've worked hard at getting your child to recognise the difference between daytime and night-time sleep by putting her down with the curtains open during the day, you should explain this to your relative – and it will help, too, if you can explain the rationale behind each point instead of just insisting, 'That's just how we do it at home'.

Treats and privileges

Explain your rationale for awarding treats and privileges: if, for example, your child has to earn privileges, or if she is restricted to one special treat per day, let Granny know; then you can establish which of you will give her that special something on a particular day. If you usually use the withdrawal of treats and privileges as a punishment, discuss how this could work at Granny's house. She may, for instance, decide to threaten the withdrawal of a treat your child usually has at home: for example, she might say that your child won't be going to the park with Mummy tomorrow unless she behaves today. Agree between you not to issue a threat unless you are both prepared to carry it out.

TV time

If you have rules as to which programmes/videos/DVDs your child can watch and which you would prefer she didn't, say so. If your relative finds this confusing, supply some DVDs or pre-recorded tapes for your child to watch. Also, discuss how long you are happy for your child to spend each day in front of the TV, and how it should be used: as an occasional treat, for example, or as a reward for great behaviour. If your relative has her own programmes she likes to watch, which your child may find boring or which may even be unsuitable, ask whether it might be possible to record them for later. Alternatively, provide some other stimulating activity for your child to enjoy alongside her granny.

Toilet habits

It can be very frustrating to get to a certain point during toilet training only for your child to revert to her old habits – and any interference in her progress is likely to result in regression. So if, for example, you've persuaded your toddler out of daytime nappies, except for when she wants to poo, explain that you would rather your relative didn't use nappies or pull-ups as an alternative to finding a loo at other times. It can be very tempting to stick a child in a nappy when she's recently trained rather than have the worry of an accident happening, so the reasons why some carers resort to this is understandable. However, if you explain that any disruption is only going to send you all back to square one, it may be easier for your relative to see your point of view. You can buy 'travel potties', which are plastic foldaway frames with disposable, absorbent liner bags, and these serve well in emergencies. The folded frame and liners will fit into a holdall or large handbag. It's helpful, too, to let your relative know of any toilet routine your child has adopted: maybe she always has a poo after meals, for instance, so that it might be better to eat lunch at home than to take a picnic to the park, at least for the time being.

Comforters

If your baby or child uses a dummy for nap times only, explain that you'd prefer it not to be offered at any other time of the day. The same goes for other comfort items, and the best thing is to stay consistent. It may be that your parent, in-law or friend has a real dislike of dummies and tries to wean your child off hers before she's ready, thinking they're doing you a favour. Pre-empt this by saying that you know their views, but that it will actually make your life much harder if they try to intervene. Point out that your child is likely to start sucking her thumb instead of having her dummy if she has to give it up before she's ready – and that this habit is far harder to break. Perhaps your relative believes in dipping a dummy into honey (or, worse still, alcohol) to help your child drop off at nap time. Neither practice is acceptable, so do make this clear from the start.

What mums say about family or friends as childminders

'My mum often says "A little of what you fancy does you good", but certain foods make Megan very hyper and have to be avoided. The other day, despite me telling Mum that Megan couldn't have orange squash, she took her to a fast-food restaurant and gave her a pint of additive-packed still orange. Megan was in a terrible state when I went to pick her up. She couldn't tell me what was wrong, but she seemed to be suffering with a headache, wouldn't eat any tea and threw herself into one tantrum after another for the rest of the evening. Mum was mortified, and I was annoyed that we all had to suffer before she would take what I said seriously.'

Jodie, 25, mum to Megan, 18 months

'My mother-in-law usually watches a lot of daytime TV, and I was a little bit worried about what Harry might be exposed to, as a lot of the shows feature

dysfunctional families shouting at each other. As it turned out, though, I needn't have worried. My mum-in-law mentioned it before I did, saying that she would record anything she really wanted to watch. She's bought lots of puzzles and toys for Harry and her to do together, and the TV only goes on if there's a good children's programme they can enjoy. I was worrying over nothing, and probably should have trusted her more in the first place.'

Norma, 31, mum to Harry, three years

'My friend Flora, who has a school-age child, thinks that kids of three sleep better at night if they don't nap during the day. At first I thought there might be some sense in this, but then Holly kept coming home over-excited and ready for anything. I told my friend that whilst I appreciated that her methods worked with her own child, they weren't right for Holly. Now, after having struggled for a couple of weeks, she's got Holly sleeping after lunch, and our bedtime routine is back to normal. Luckily Flora's a really good friend and didn't mind me insisting on my own way.'

Helena, 28, mum to Holly, three years

'My mate, Mike, is a full-time househusband who cares for his own 21-month-old son at home. I wasn't sure how he'd cope with Jack, too, but I am really amazed at how much I've learned from him! Men come at things from a totally different perspective, and although, to my mind, he lets Jack get away with murder, Jack knows exactly where the lines are drawn and has total respect for Mike. I think it's because he has so much freedom that he's ready to respond to the word "no" when it does come. Mike's methods

are starting to work for me at home, too, now that I've learned to be a bit more relaxed around Jack.'

Gemma, 27, mum to Jack, 21 months

Keeping your side of the bargain

Don't forget that any contract – however informal and whether written or verbal – has two sides to it, and you have an obligation to keep to your side, too. It's tempting, for instance, to regard your relative as someone you can take advantage of – perhaps by asking her to hang on to your child for a bit longer so you can go for a drink after work, or by arriving extra early for the drop-off one morning so you can attend a meeting. These things may well be negotiable – but there's the watchword: 'negotiable'. If you are going to require extra hours, you need to give plenty of notice and make the request in the same way as you would ask a paid childminder. It's important that you don't automatically expect the answer 'yes', too. Your relative should feel relaxed enough about your arrangement to be comfortable about declining – even if it seems she has no other plans. She may love looking after her grandchild very much, but she may also genuinely need time to recover, or just feel that she wants her evenings to herself.

To pay or not to pay?

That is, indeed, the question for many families whose relatives or friends are their main childcarers. In many cases a nominal fee, agreed by both parties, works well: the relative doesn't feel put upon, and is more likely to stick to your 'rules'; you, on the other hand, feel more in control and less indebted. One way of working out an amount is to make your relative an offer at the top end of what you would be happy to pay (which will be less than formal registered childcare); then, if they refuse or come in with a much lower amount, agree on a payment halfway between. This way you are still getting a bargain and they feel valued. If, on the other hand, they accept your first offer, you are still only paying what you know you can afford.

If financial remuneration is out of the question, however – perhaps because either side feels uncomfortable with it or because you simply can't afford to pay anything – there are still ways of giving something back, and it's especially important that you do make gestures of appreciation if no money will be changing hands.

How to show your appreciation

The most memorable gestures are those that have been carefully thought out: a bunch of flowers from the petrol station's forecourt may be received gratefully enough, but a little something – and it doesn't have to cost much – that has been planned specifically with your carer in mind will go a long way to making her feel appreciated. Think about what, for example, she may be giving up in order to provide childcare for you. Perhaps she has swapped a regular afternoon shopping with friends, or a coffee morning at a social club for time spent looking after your child? In this case, give her advance warning that you are taking a day or a morning off work so that she can have some time to herself; encourage her to organise a coffee morning at home for her friends, then turn up in advance with a couple of lovely cakes or some fresh raspberries and cream as a special treat. Maybe she has less time to herself than before? Treat her to a manicure or a facial at the weekend, or find out when your department store is holding their next free makeover session, then leave your child with your partner and take her out for a girly make-up and shopping trip.

A handwritten note or 'thank you' card from time to time – or something your child has helped to make – will also be treasured by your relative, and is worth more than money to many grandparents. Similarly, a few well-chosen words of thanks will mean a lot: why not remind your mum, if she is your child's carer, of how good a job she did when you were little? Saying something such as 'I used to love the way you read bedtime stories to me' or 'I felt really loved as a child' are huge compliments that cost nothing to say. (Imagine how proud you would feel if your child could articulate a sentiment like that now!)

When one side feels pushed out

Some lucky families are able to split the childcare arrangements between both sets of grandparents, and they are fortunate indeed. Of course, there can be problems when your child clearly prefers one set to the other, or where one set does more hours than the other, and this is when your skills of diplomacy are likely to be tested to their limits.

It's a good idea to agree in advance what sorts of activities each set will do with your child (making sure you allot some of your child's favourites to each). Your parents, for instance, may want to take your child to the park once or twice a week. Your in-laws, on the other hand, could be in charge of library trips or a weekly treat at the baker's or sweet shop. In other words, making sure that your child looks forward specifically to at least one or two elements of each care arrangement will mean that she is less likely to show a preference for either. If your child seems to prefer one granny's cooking to the other's, it might be better for her to take a packed lunch to each from time to time, or for you to provide puddings, for instance.

If one set of grandparents lives at a distance or cannot be involved in regular childcare for whatever reason, you can help them to feel more involved by making more of an effort to see them – either at your place or theirs – and perhaps setting up some holiday childcare for them to get involved in. Perhaps they could come and stay in your home for a week or so during the summer holidays and care for your child? If your child is willing, maybe they could take her away with them for a few days or care for her in their own home? If none of this is practical, do try to send them photographs of your child regularly, and get your child to create little pieces of 'artwork' you can forward. It's even more important for you to express your appreciation of them as grandparents if their noses are likely to be out of joint because the other side of the family's involvement is greater – however unavoidable this might be.

Pros

- Grandparents will love your child unconditionally.
- They are experienced parents themselves.
- They may be prepared to drop off and collect from pre-school, school or nursery.
- They may agree to attend your usual mother-and-baby or toddler groups with your child.
- They may be happy for your child to have friends round to play.
- They may agree to the odd sleepover to make your days less frantic.
- They will probably look after your child even when she is sick.
- All these points may also apply to other relatives and friends.

Cons

- Depending on their age and fitness, grandparents may have less energy than other childcare providers.
- They may be out of touch with modern parenting methods.
- They don't have to provide educational activities and probably won't have any formal qualifications to do so.
- You may need to buy a second set of baby or toddler equipment for their home, and put household safety measures in place.

- They may be inclined to 'spoil' your child, despite your protests.
- If things don't work out, it could cause a family rift.
- All these points may also apply to other relatives and friends.

Clever answers to tricky questions

Here are some of the questions other mums have had to field from their parents, friends and in-laws, plus information to help you to answer them.

They say: 'I gave you sweets every day when you were little, so why can't I give them to my own grandchild?'

You say: 'There wasn't so much public information available about general nutrition, childhood obesity, dental health, additives and colourants back then. Research has proven that certain additives and high levels of sugar in sweets can cause disruptive behaviour in children. As an occasional treat they're fine, but not as an everyday food.'

They say: 'What's wrong with crisps as a morning snack? She says she doesn't like fruit, and she's got to eat something.'

You say: 'She knows that fruit is the only option when she's at home, so she generally tends to eat it. If she refuses it, she knows there's nothing else until lunchtime. If she gets hungry in the meantime she's allowed a small glass of milk. The high salt and fat content in crisps makes children crave them, but the nutritional value is so poor that she's better off with nothing at all.'

They say: 'Don't home-fried chips count as one portion of the five fruit and veg he should be eating?

You say: 'No. Chips – home-cooked or not – don't count as a portion of vegetables because potatoes are classed nutritionally as a carbohydrate. In any case, deep-frying any food increases its fat content to way above what would be considered healthy by a nutritionist. Enough foods are fat-laden as it is without us offering kids foods that have been specially cooked in fat.'

They say: 'Once she's gone down for her nap, she stays asleep for up to three hours at a time and I don't like to wake her.'

You say: 'Unless she's unwell or has had disrupted sleep the previous night, wake her after two hours at most – this is plenty of daytime sleep for a young child (most nap for one to two hours). If she stays asleep for longer there's a good chance she won't sleep well at bedtime.'

They say: 'Why does he need to go outdoors in the winter? He'll only catch a cold.'

You say: 'More and more children are becoming obese because of their sedentary lifestyle, which is why kids need to exercise for some part of each day, all year round. As long as he is wearing warm clothes and a hat, he won't catch a cold and, unless it's icy, it should be safe to venture outside. Colds are caught by ingesting saliva from an infected person (from close contact, a sneeze or a cough, for instance), not from feeling cold – although there's some research to suggest that the immune system doesn't function so efficiently when we're chilled, leaving us less able to fight infections, so he needs to wrap up warmly.'

They say: 'Why is she still in nappies? I had you toilet-trained at 18 months!'

You say: 'There are still some experts who advocate early potty training, but it's often more by luck than judgement that a child performs on a potty this early. In any case, studies show that if you wait until your child shows signs of readiness, she'll have fewer accidents (which could damage her confidence) and a much quicker result overall.'

What friends and family say about being childminders

'We waited a long time for Jacob to arrive as our daughter, Niamh, was 38 when she had him. He's our only grandchild, so although my husband and I are both in our seventies now, we are only too pleased to be able to care for him, and I'd much rather he was with family than in a nursery where he doesn't know anyone. We are both fairly fit and energetic, so we're coping well, despite the fact that Jacob runs rings round us! At least we are both retired, so we can take it in turns to have a rest.'

Eleanor, 71, grandmother to Jacob, two

'Our son and his wife are always trying to press money on me for looking after Sarah-Louise, but I don't want payment – she's my grand-daughter! Besides, I did the same for my other grandchildren, so I'm used to having youngsters around the place. I have Sarah-Louise for four hours every weekday, and most of the time it's a joy, although I won't pretend

it's not hard work. Little things my daughter-in-law does, like buying me a special bunch of flowers or a tin of fancy biscuits now and then, mean a lot to me – but I'd be happy caring for the baby anyway.'

Diana, 59, grandmother to Sarah-Louise, six months

'I was really excited to be asked to help out looking after my best friend Lucie's son, Adam, three days a week. He's a real cutie, he gets on well with my own son and we have a lovely relationship. Lucie wouldn't hear of not paying me, but I wouldn't take any money, so she gives me supermarket vouchers or a few bags of essential groceries now and then. She's even booked me in for a haircut and colour, which I was struggling to afford. It works out really well because I don't feel at all put upon and Lucie isn't tied to giving me a fixed amount of money every week, so the whole arrangement is very flexible and suits us both.'

Julie, mum to Harry, 10 months, and
minder to Adam, 15 months

Useful contacts for grandparent childcarers

If your parents or in-laws are thinking about caring for your children full-time, they will find advice and support at the Grandparents Association advice line on 0845 4349585, or at Parentline Plus (freephone 0808 800 2222).

Chapter 5

How to choose childcare

One of the most daunting prospects when it comes to finding childcare can be deciding which type will best suit your needs and those of your child. 'Fitting the childcare to the child isn't an exact science,' says chartered educational psychologist Dr Richard Woolfson. 'Sometimes, for example, a quiet child thrives best in a quiet context with only a few other children, whereas a different quiet child may develop social skills very quickly in a socially challenging environment. It makes most sense, at the outset, to be led by your instincts.'

All the talk of nannies versus nurseries and childminders versus au pairs can be mind-boggling enough, but ultimately you will probably have to narrow it down to one choice – or, in some cases, a combination of two or more. Here's a technique for helping you to shortlist your choices – although before you try it, make sure you have familiarised yourself with Chapter 3. Consider each question from the section 'What are your needs?' (overleaf), marking each answer with a tick under the relevant childcare provider(s) in the chart on page 91. Whichever providers have the most ticks at the end of the questionnaire may be the ones most suited to your family's needs.

What are your needs?

Here are lists of things to ask yourself before you research specific types of childcare.

Location

Bear in mind that you may need to consider these points also if you will be using a combination of childcare – say, for instance, your parents or in-laws as well as a day nursery.

- Would you prefer for your child to be looked after in your own home? If your answer is 'yes', mark a tick under 'nanny', 'au pair' and, if applicable, 'parents/in-laws/friends' on page 91.
- Does your childcare provision need to be local to your home or close to your work? Mark a tick next to each type of provision you know exists close to your preferred location.
- Should your provider be located close to a mainline railway station or along a bus or underground route? Mark a tick next to each type of provision that is close by.
- If you are driving to drop off and pick up your child, is there adequate parking? Mark a tick next to each type of provision with convenient parking nearby.

Your child

- Does your child have special needs? (See page 115.) Mark a tick next to each provider you know has, or think may have, experience in this area.
- Is your child gregarious or shy? (And would you prefer to nurture this trait in him or encourage him

more the other way?) If he is shy, for example, you might prefer to place him in a closer-knit, more homely provision such as with a childminder or family or friend, in which case mark a tick against each of these; if you would prefer him to be in a more bustling, busy environment, mark a tick against day nursery, pre-school/playgroup, Sure Start Children's Centre and nursery school/class.

- Does your child fare better in small or large groups? Mark a tick next to each type of provision that you believe will offer the optimum group size.
- Would you prefer your child to mix with children his own age or a broader range of ages? Mark a tick next to each type of provision that you believe will offer the optimum age range.
- Does your child adapt well to new adults and situations? If not, mark a tick next to parents/in-laws/friend and, possibly, childminder.
- Would your child be happier with just one adult taking full responsibility for his care? If so, mark a tick next to parents/in-laws/friend, childminder and, if appropriate, nanny and au pair.

Environment

- Would you prefer your child to be cared for in a home environment? If so, mark a tick next to parents/in-laws/friend, childminder and, if appropriate, nanny and au pair.
- Is your child used to mixing with large groups of children and adults? If so, you might choose to put a tick next to day nursery, pre-school/playgroup, Sure Start Children's Centre and nursery school/class.

- Is your child likely to prefer a structured 'classroom' set-up to a 'free play' environment? If so, mark a tick next to day nursery, pre-school and nursery school/class. If not, tick the other options.
- Would you prefer your child's day to be centred more around education or recreation? Mark a tick next to the providers that you believe will provide the more appropriate activities.

The childcarer

- Would you prefer more than one adult to be responsible for your child's care? If so, mark a tick next to day nursery, pre-school playgroup, Sure Start Children's Centre and nursery school/class.
- Would you prefer more opportunities for one-to-one care? If so, mark a tick next to childminder; parents/in-laws/friend and, if appropriate, nanny and au pair.
- Does the childcarer need to be qualified? If so, mark a tick against all providers except parents/in-laws/friend and au pair.
- Would you prefer the carer to be a parent him- or herself? If so, mark a tick against any providers that you know are parents.
- Is it important to you that the carer will follow the Early Years Foundation Stage curriculum laid down by the government for all children aged from birth to five? If so, mark a tick next to all providers except parents/in-laws/friend, out-of-school care, nanny and au pair. (Most pre-schools and playgroups now follow the Early Years Foundation Stage.)

Other practicalities

- Are you likely to need short-notice emergency cover? If so, a childminder, parent/in-law/friend, nanny or au pair will probably be the most flexible.
- Are your childcare requirements sporadic or fixed? If they are sporadic, a parent/in-law/friend is likely to be your best bet.
- Will you need cover during school holiday times? If so, day nurseries, Sure Start Children's Centres, childminders and, if applicable, nannies and au pairs are able to offer this.
- Do you need your provider to cover office hours and travelling time? If so, day nurseries, Sure Start Children's Centres, childminders, out-of-school care and, if applicable, nannies and au pairs may be able to offer this.

Mark your ticks in the right-hand column	
Au pair	
Childminder	
Day nursery	
Nanny	
Nursery school/class	
Out-of-school care	
Parents/in-laws/friend	
Pre-school/playgroup	
Sure Start Children's Centre	

Where to look

So where on earth is all this childcare provision? Chances are that before you became a parent you lived in blissful ignorance of all the childcare providers around you, but now it has become a priority to find out what's available locally that meets your requirements. A good starting point is to approach your local Children's Information Services (CIS), which hold lists of all registered childcare provision in your area (see page 178). They won't recommend one provider over another, but it's just as well to have some kind of directory you can begin working from. Your local library may hold a similar list, although it may not be as comprehensive as the CIS database.

Another place to try is your GP's surgery, especially if yours is a health centre where midwives or health visitors hold clinics. Sometimes your midwife or health visitor may recommend a particular childminder or nursery to you, but more often they will just point you in the right direction of finding something close by. If you are a member of the National Childbirth Trust (NCT), your local group leader may also be able to help (see page 180). Some families find the NCT a great source of all-round support, especially in the early days of new parenthood.

Word of mouth is always invaluable in circumstances like these, so ask around amongst friends, family, antenatal or postnatal groups. Even first-time mums may have sisters or cousins locally who can make a recommendation. It's also worth becoming a member of one of the websites for parents so that you can bounce ideas off other mums via the forums. Try www.ukparents.co.uk or www.netmums.co.uk, for instance. If you register with your local Netmums group, you'll find information about local resources as well as getting a chance for a webchat with other mums in your neighbourhood. This can be of real value if you're new to the area or don't know many people in your situation.

What each type of childcare could offer your child

Once you have narrowed down your choices regarding different types of childcare, the next step is to consider what each option can offer your child in terms of pastoral and social development, stimulation, intellectual development and behaviour. It's important to match your child to the childcare that suits him best in as many of these categories as possible. The experience of childcare will stay with him for many years to come – possibly all his life – and happy memories laid down at this stage will form great building blocks for later on.

Start by making appointments to view a few examples of each of your shortlisted options, and go prepared to conduct a mini interview at each. It will help you to focus if you go armed with a list of questions to ask in each situation, and you'll find suggestions for these below each section in this chapter. Make sure at the time of booking your appointment that the appropriate person will be in attendance, and that enough time has been set aside (say half an hour) for you to make a thorough assessment of the provision. Ask to be shown all around every part of the premises that your child will use, including toilets and sleeping areas. It's a good idea to ask to see the kitchens, too, especially if food is prepared on the premises.

Don't be afraid to make at least one unscheduled return visit: plan to drop in at a different time of day on each occasion so that you can see what else goes on and how the children seem to be behaving. It's best to avoid mealtimes, though, as these are very busy for the staff, and children tend to eat better without extra distractions.

Day nursery

Whilst your child won't enjoy as much one-to-one attention in a day nursery as in some other types of childcare, his personal, social and educational development will be the focus of his time spent there. Because nursery days are structured, he will benefit from a regular routine, and the need to share and cooperate should help him to make friends, consider others and become adept at teamwork and play. There is usually some one-to-one interaction between child and key worker each day, and the atmosphere in nurseries is usually lively and stimulating, although there are pre-set quiet times in addition to the usual nap times, too.

A good nursery will structure its days to maximise the children's potential, stimulating them and optimising attention spans at times when they have the most energy; providing quiet play or a story towards nap times and again as the day draws to a close. A good indicator of a well-organised nursery is a forward planner on display for parents to see which activities are planned for when in the coming weeks; similarly, menus for the week should be on display or easily accessible. These measures demonstrate that staff are engaging in mid- to long-term planning, and enable parents to check that the nursery is embracing the Early Years Foundation Stage curriculum.

The nursery manager should be able to describe how the curriculum is covered through various activities spanning the week. There should be a good mix of activities each day to stimulate and develop the children physically and mentally, including role play, sensory hands-on exploration, creative play, number work, letter formation, physical activities and story telling.

What to ask at a nursery

If your child is a baby:

- Are dummies and other comforters allowed?
- Can you store and reheat breastmilk?
- Which formula milks are used?
- Which types of bottle are used?
- May I bring in my own bottles if the shape/teat doesn't suit my baby?
- What if he won't sleep at nap time?
- What if he cries continuously and won't settle?
- Who will change my baby's nappy?
- Will my baby be changed as soon as he soils his nappy or are nappy changes scheduled for pre-set times?

If your child is a toddler:

- What's the policy on discipline?
- What's the policy on undesirable habits (e.g. biting, hair-pulling and so on)?
- How is toilet training managed?

- Does the nursery feed on to a particular primary school?
- What if my child is unhappy?
- What if he refuses to eat?
- What if he won't sleep at nap times?
- What if he can't make friends?

General questions

- What 'settling-in' routine and period do you have?
- What happens in case of injury?
- What happens if my child falls ill?
- How do staff prevent unauthorised entry into the building?
- What security measures are in place?
- Does a 'key worker' scheme operate, where one carer takes overall responsibility for my child?
- What if he doesn't bond with his key worker?
- Is there a daily record book via which key workers and parents can communicate?
- What is the ratio of carers to children? (Remember, this should be one carer for every three under-twos; one carer for every four two-year-olds and one carer for every eight children over the age of two.)
- Where will my child eat and sleep?
- What play equipment, books and other facilities are available?
- What outdoor play facilities are available?

- What is the daily routine?
- Are meals prepared on the premises or bought in from an outside source?
- Do meals contain additives or GM (genetically modified) ingredients?
- Do you cater for special dietary needs or fussy eaters?
- Can staff administer prescribed or other medicines?
- How fast is staff turnover?
- Are there financial penalties if I am late collecting my child?
- How can parents become more involved with the nursery?
- Are there any circumstances in which you would not allow my child to attend?
- Can you put me in touch with other parents who use your facility?

What to ask yourself

- Do the nursery and its staff feel welcoming?
- Do the children look happy and purposeful?
- Are they well supervised?
- Are there examples of the children's work on display?
- Are the premises clean, bright and spacious?
- Are the relevant insurance, registration and Ofsted inspection documents on display?
- Are there fire precautions in evidence?

Pre-school or playgroup

As pre-schools and playgroups generally offer places for children aged three to five years (although some will take two-year-olds), this isn't the choice for you if you have a baby. For toddlers, though, it can offer a really good grounding for school, especially if your child is happy to mix with boys and girls who may be a little older or younger than he is. Your child will usually begin the first stage of the National Curriculum, called the 'Foundation Stage', and this focuses on the needs of children from age three until they reach the end of the reception year of primary school.

The curriculum is delivered through planned play activities, which should encourage all children to reach their individual potential. Skills taught include clarity of speech, listening, tenacity, early reading, writing and numeracy. The aim is for the children to achieve or even exceed the early learning goals laid down by the curriculum by the end of the 'Foundation Stage', giving them the best possible start for school.

Most pre-school groups accommodate up to 20 children at a time, although some take fewer. They should be registered with Ofsted and inspected regularly. Inspection covers all aspects of the childcare on offer, including the safety and suitability of the buildings.

What to ask at a pre-school or playgroup

- How many children do you care for?
- What is the ratio of staff to children? (There should be one member of staff for every eight children

aged three to five, and one for every four children aged two.)

- What safety measures are in place?
- How do you prevent unauthorised access to the building?
- What qualifications do staff members hold?
- What 'settling-in' routine and period do you have?
- What if my child doesn't settle?
- What if he doesn't bond with staff?
- What if my child struggles with the curriculum?
- What is your policy on discipline?
- What's the policy on undesirable habits (e.g. biting, hair pulling and so on)?
- Do you keep a daily record of my child's progress?
- What if my child is unhappy?
- What if he finds it hard to make friends?
- What if he falls ill?
- What happens in case of injury?
- What play equipment, books and other facilities are available?
- What outdoor play facilities are available?
- What is the daily routine?
- Can staff administer prescribed or other medicines?
- How fast is staff turnover?

- Are there any circumstances in which you would not allow my child to attend?
- Can you put me in touch with other parents who use your facility?

What to ask yourself

- Do the group and its staff feel welcoming?
- Do the children look happy and absorbed?
- Are they well supervised?
- Are there examples of the children's work on display?
- Are the premises clean, bright and spacious?
- Are the relevant insurance, registration and Ofsted inspection documents on display?
- Are there fire precautions in evidence?

Childminder

For most parents, the main benefit of hiring a childminder is that their baby or child will be cared for in a home environment with few other children. Apart from using parents, in-laws or friends as carers (see later in the chapter), this is probably the closest environment your child can experience to staying in his own home. It can be a good choice for children who are intimidated by larger groups or who find it more difficult than others to fall into a routine. For babies, the informality may mean more flexibility about feeding, sleeping and nappy-changing times, as well as other activities during the day.

Now that childminders are expected to have completed courses in early years education, and to adhere to the government's Early Learning Foundation Stage curriculum for babies and pre-schoolers, the standard of care is higher than ever, and your baby or child will be formally encouraged in his development as well as being looked after.

If well-kept and well-equipped, a childminder's home can offer enough challenges for your baby or child to practise many skills, and a good-sized garden or nearby park should be available for outdoor play, fresh air and letting off steam.

Childminders are able to care for babies from newborn, as well as toddlers and older children, although they can only care for up to three children under the age of five (including their own) at any one time, as well as three older children. This could mean, of course, that a childminder could be caring for three babies at once. Whilst this would give your baby the opportunity to socialise with other infants his age, it could be difficult for the childminder to pay a lot of one-to-one attention to each.

What to ask a childminder
If your child is a baby:

- How many babies are in your care?
- How many other children are in your care, and how old are they?
- How do you ensure that each baby/child gets individual attention?

- What do you do when more than one baby is crying at the same time?
- Where and when will my baby sleep?
- What if he won't stop crying?
- When would you call the doctor?
- What safety measures are in place (stairgates, cupboard locks, fire extinguishers, etc.)?

If your child is a toddler:

- What early learning activities will you be engaging my child in?
- What happens if he doesn't get on with the other children in your care?
- How would you deal with a tantrum?
- What is your approach to discipline generally?
- What if my child won't sleep?
- What if he won't eat?
- How do you approach toilet training?

General questions:

- Why did you become a childminder?
- How long have you been doing it?
- What do you like best about childminding?
- May I see your registration and public liability insurance documents?
- May I see your first-aid certificate?

- May I see evidence that you and any other adults who use the house have passed CRB checks?
- Have you done any extra training?
- Are all the rooms and outdoor spaces insured for my child to use?
- How do you spend your days with the children?
- Do you use the TV/DVD player as a diversion? If so, for how long per day?
- Who else comes and goes in the house when the children are here?
- Do you – or does anyone else who uses the house – smoke?
- Do you keep a file on each child's progress?
- What kind of food and drinks do you provide and are meals homemade?
- Do you take the children out?
- Do you have pets?
- Do you drive? If so, do you have a clean licence?
- Do you have properly fitted car seats?
- Do you offer a trial period?
- Are there any circumstances in which you would not allow my child to attend?
- Can you put me in touch with other parents who use your facility?

What to ask yourself

- Do the childminder and her home feel welcoming?
- Do you feel you could get on with the childminder?
- Is her home clean, tidy and well kept?
- Does it smell of pets or cigarette smoke?
- Are all the usual safety devices in place?
- Are the toys, books and other playthings well organised?
- Is there plenty of space for playing and moving about?
- Is the sleeping area cosy and conducive to sleep?
- Are there fire precautions in evidence?

Nursery school or class

Nursery schools and classes offer a slightly more formal approach to learning than pre-school groups and are usually open during school hours, offering half-day or full-day sessions. Like pre-schools, they take children from three (or sometimes two) up to five years, so if you're looking for childcare from age two onwards, this would certainly give your child continuity of care, especially if he attends a nursery school attached to the primary that you are hoping he will attend. It will also give him the opportunity to make friends that he may start school with later on, which helps to make the transition to school smoother and less traumatic all round.

Nursery schools and classes are headed up by trained teachers and regularly inspected by Ofsted; they also follow the Early Years Foundation Stage curriculum laid down by the government.

Some nursery schools also offer out-of-school care, so when your child reaches school age you might want to investigate the possibility of him transferring from his class to the out-of-school provision at the end of each school day. Even if your nursery school or class is part of the state system, you will be expected to pay for this extra provision (see Chapter 3 for more details).

It may be worth considering a nursery school or class for your child if he seems to thrive on continuity: even if the staff change, the environment is unlikely to, and there will usually be other staff he knows in attendance. The downside could be that your child will be effectively 'institutionalised' within the school system from the age of two or three. Also, if he is to start school, then go on to out-of-school care afterwards, this can seem like a very long time to be away from a home or home-like environment.

What to ask at a nursery school/class

- How many children will be the same age as my child?
- What if he won't cooperate with your curriculum activities?
- What if he doesn't bond with staff?
- Do you allow for daytime naps? If so, where do the children sleep?

- Do you allow for children who aren't yet toilet-trained?
- How do you manage toilet training?
- Who will change my child's nappy/trainer pants?
- Are there opportunities for outdoor play?
- Do you go out on trips? If so, where to and how often?
- How many staff are there? (Remember, there should be at least one adult per 10–13 children.)
- Do you have a 'settling-in' routine and period?
- What if my child can't settle?
- Do you keep a daily record of the children's progress?
- How do you encourage friendships to develop?
- Can you use any of the school's facilities (where the nursery is attached to a primary school)?
- What if my child falls ill?
- Are there any circumstances in which you would not allow my child to attend?
- Can you put me in touch with other parents who use your facility?

What to ask yourself

- Do the nursery school/class and its staff feel welcoming?
- Do the children look happy and purposeful?
- Are they being well supervised and controlled?
- Are examples of their work on display?

- Is all the play equipment, including toys, well organised and well kept?
- Are the premises clean, bright and spacious?
- Are the relevant insurance, registration and Ofsted inspection documents on display?
- Are there fire precautions in evidence?

Out-of-school care

Schoolchildren who attend out-of-school childcare sessions – which are held in some nurseries, schools, community centres or youth clubs – usually have access to a wide range of activities, including music, art clubs, sports or homework support groups. Some parents combine out-of-school care for their school-age child with another type of provision, such as a childminder or grandparent carer. Others use the holiday play schemes, which run out of term time and are usually open from around 8 a.m. to 6 p.m. Leaders and at least half the helpers must be trained or qualified in some relevant way.

Out-of-school childcare providers are registered and subject to Ofsted inspections if the children are up to eight years old and if the centre is open for more than two hours per day for six or more days per year. Clubs offering provision for children exclusively over the age of eight don't need to be registered, but they may have opted to be 'quality assured' under a government-run scheme, so it's worth asking.

Your child may enjoy out-of-school care if he is gregarious and doesn't mind loud noise and large groups of mixed-age children. If he is happier in a quieter, home environment, it might be better to consider a childminder, friend or relative as an out-of-school carer.

What to ask at an out-of-school club

- How many children usually attend?
- What activities are on offer?
- Are there any extra costs involved in the activities?
- Is there help with homework? If so, where do the children work?
- What qualifications do the leader and other staff have?
- Is there a quieter place for younger children to go?
- What happens in case of an emergency?
- What if my child falls ill?
- What if he is unhappy?
- What are the security arrangements?
- How much one-to-one attention does each child get?
- Is a record kept of each child's progress?
- Can you put me in touch with other parents who use your facility?

What to ask yourself

- Do the centre and its staff feel welcoming?
- Do the children appear to be happy and occupied?
- Are they well supervised?

- Is the place well organised?
- Are the facilities well maintained?
- Are the premises clean, bright and spacious?
- Are the relevant insurance, registration and Ofsted inspection documents on display?
- Are there fire precautions in evidence?

Nanny

A nanny can be a good childcare choice if your child prefers to form close one-to-one bonds with people rather than mix in with a larger group of adults and children – and if he does enjoy the company of others sometimes, a nanny can take him to mother-and-toddler or other local groups for outside activities. In fact, a recent survey found that a nanny would be the preferred childcare choice of 82% of working mums if only this were an affordable option. Although nannies don't have to be registered and are not regulated, they can choose to become 'approved' through the government's Childcare Approval Scheme, and this is an accreditation worth looking for, although it will be down to you to check out any credentials offered by a potential nanny.

One of the great advantages of nanny care is that it's home-based, so your child will remain surrounded by all his own familiar things. He's more likely to relax and sleep in his own home than in less familiar surroundings and probably has access to many more toys, books and other playthings than with any other kind of provision (with the exception of relatives or friends if they are coming to your home to care for your child).

Childcare that's based in your own home means no early-morning waking and rushing around for your child, and no mad panic for you to get back bang on time in the evening. Also, if your child is unwell, your nanny will still care for him. This is a great weight off many working parents' minds: the same survey found that only 23% are allowed paid leave if their child is ill, yet most nurseries will not allow infectious children to attend.

Nannies can be a wholly unknown quantity unless you have inherited a nanny from a friend or neighbour, or you are embarking on a nanny share where another family already knows the nanny. For this reason, it's important to interview prospective nannies thoroughly – and a good candidate will expect nothing less. After all, if successful, she will have sole care of your child for long hours at a time, so she should be just as keen for you to know that she is honest, trustworthy and capable as you are yourself.

It's a good idea to arrange for a short preliminary chat on the phone before inviting a prospective nanny to come for a more formal interview. This will allow you both to get a feel for each other and see if you can establish a rapport. When you are ready to meet face to face, prepare your interview questions ahead of time, making sure to include all the points below, whether or not the nanny has been recommended by someone you know. Keep a pen and paper handy to jot down pertinent answers. Allow time, too, for the interviewee to ask you questions (and be a bit wary if she doesn't appear to have anything she wants to find out about you and your family). Let her know that, if she is shortlisted, you would like her to come back and spend some time with your child before you make a final decision. This way you can observe how she interacts with your child and assess whether or not they are likely to get on with each other.

Remember that however well qualified a prospective nanny may be on paper, a sunny disposition, proven ability and a genuine enjoyment of children are equally important, if not more so.

What to ask a nanny

- Why did you decide to become a nanny?
- How much experience do you have?
- What was your last job and why did you leave?
- What is your current position and why do you want to leave?
- Talk me through each of your jobs and why you left.
- What are you looking for in your next position?
- Do you prefer to live in or out?
- What do you enjoy about looking after children?
- How would you spend your days with my child?
- What ideas do you have for rainy-day play?
- Can you cook?
- What meals could you prepare for my child?
- How could you help my child with weaning, self-feeding, potty training, reading and writing?
- What are your views on children and sweets, TV programmes, computer games, etc?

- Do you smoke?
- What would you do in the event of a family crisis? (Think up an example before the interview.)
- How do you respond generally to stressful situations?
- What difficulties have you experienced with previous families and how were they resolved?
- What is your own family background?
- Where does your family live?
- What particular childcare skills do you believe you have?
- What training in childcare and development have you had?
- What other qualifications do you have?
- Do you have plans to gain further qualifications?
- How many days have you had off sick in the last 12 months?
- Are you trained in first aid? How would you control a high fever? Respond to a choking fit?
- How do you see your role in disciplining my child?
- Which methods of discipline work best for you?
- When did you pass your driving test? Can you show me a full, clean driving licence?
- Do you have your own car?
- Are you insured to take my child out in your car?
- What salary are you seeking?

- When would you be available to start a new position?
- Would you accept the position if it were offered to you?

Add in other questions, where relevant, or adapt these to suit your own family situation. It might help if you rate each interviewee's answers to the questions on a scale of 1–3, then total her scores at the end. This can act as an aide-memoire when it comes to drawing up a shortlist, recalling individuals and assessing their overall suitability.

Au pair

As described in Chapter 3, this option is not for you unless your child is at least three years old. Some of the advantages of nanny care are also offered by au pairs, but their working hours are greatly limited by comparison, and they need no training or experience. There are restrictions as to where your au pair can originate from and his or her marital status, amongst other matters (see page 156).

The plus points are that your au pair will live in your home, so there is no need for a frantic morning routine to get your child to his childcarer, and your child will be surrounded by his own things and can feel relaxed in his own home.

Advantages over nannies are that au pairs are expected to do light housework as well as childcare, and to provide two evenings' babysitting per week, which is included in their pay; and the cost to you of hiring an au pair is minimal compared with any other form of childcare.

Language may be a barrier, but this more commonly affects the relationship between parents and au pair than the relationship with the child. Children can be very inventive, and will come up with new words or gestures to indicate their needs or what they are trying to communicate; they are also often very quick to pick up new languages themselves and may understand their au pair more quickly and easily than you do.

As au pairs are only permitted to work for up to five hours per day, five days per week, you may have to dovetail this with out-of-school care or childcare from parents, in-laws or friends if you work regular hours. Bear in mind also that most au pairs stay with one family for only around six months, and the turnover can be even faster than that: not only will this mean you might have gaps in your childcare, but you may also have to interview regularly, and your child's bond with his carer will be broken each time.

What to ask an au pair

Basically, the list of questions to ask a nanny are interchangeable with those for an au pair interview, but with a few of the questions omitted. It's probably wise to try to get some commitment out of your prospective au pair as to how long she's likely to stay. Because she's unlikely to have any childcare qualifications, you might want to spend more time questioning her about her own home life: did she have younger brothers, sisters or cousins to care for? Find out, too, whether she has any particular skills she could share with your child: is she a good singer or a keen swimmer? Can she play a musical instrument or coach him in a sport?

Keeping an open mind

Although you have had the opportunity now to narrow things down a bit and may have already decided which types of childcare to investigate more fully, do try to keep an open mind. You might have decided, for example, that a day nursery sounds just the right type of childcare for you and your child, only to discover that the waiting list in your area is unfeasibly long; you might have dismissed using your parents and/or friends as carers, but then find that you aren't happy with any of the paid care currently available in your area; perhaps your chosen carer can put you on a waiting list with a view to offering you a place a few months after you require it, but you'll need some interim help.

Whatever the stumbling block – if you do encounter one – it will pay to have a second choice as back-up. Perhaps you could enlist the services of an alternative provider until such a time as your preferred option becomes available; in this case, though, do bear in mind that your child may well settle down with the first arrangement and then find it too disruptive to be moved.

Finding care for children with special needs

We have already established that high-quality childcare can be beneficial to all children and their families, and this includes children with special needs or disabilities. In fact, enrolling a child with special educational needs into good pre-school provision may even reduce the need for intervention later on at school.

The general principles for choosing and maintaining a childcare setting apply as much to a child with special needs as they do to a typically developing child. For children with physical disabilities, childcare can provide opportunities for acceptance and for integration with able-bodied children. The younger we introduce children to others with physical, mental or educational disabilities, the greater their acceptance is likely to be. Since raising a disabled child can, in some instances, cost a great deal more than raising an able child, there's yet more emphasis on parents returning to work. And even if one or both parents stay home to care for their child, they may still need regular breaks from their caring duties, and quality childcare can provide the answer.

Some areas may have childcare services especially tailored for children with disabilities and special educational needs; in others, these services are inclusive within existing childcare provision. In some places, for instance, there are childminding networks whose minders have had special training to work with children with disabilities and special needs. Contact your local Children's Information Service or the National Childminding Association for more details (see pages 178 and 180).

All day nurseries, which are legally obliged to be registered, have a designated Special Educational Needs Coordinator (SENCO) to coordinate provision for children with special needs, so ask to be put in touch with the relevant person when you investigate each nursery option.

Talk to potential childcare providers about your child's specific needs. Does he have any special dietary or physiotherapy requirements? Does he need to be given regular medications? If so, how can each provider accommodate these needs?

It's worth visiting the government's public services website at www.direct.gov.uk or approaching your local council direct, as some councils have funding set aside specifically for assisting children with special needs or disabilities. This could mean, for instance, that extra staff or equipment could be given to a local childcare provider to enable you to take up a place that would otherwise prove unsuitable.

It is illegal for childcare providers to discriminate against children with special needs or disabilities. This means, for example, that they can't refuse to take a disabled child on an organised outing or charge you more without a proven financial reason. They must also undertake to make 'reasonable adjustments' to their services and facilities so they are suitable for use by disabled children. When choosing childcare, parents should also ensure that the staff have a good understanding of their child's specific developmental needs and ensure that they can adapt and tailor their programme of activities to his development level instead of delivering it at his age level. A childcare setting that has previous experience of caring for children with special needs can draw on that to support children who currently have special needs. For a list of contacts, see page 177.

Chapter 6

How to get the best out of childcare

Once you've chosen and organised your childcare there is much you can do to optimise the experience for you and your child, from getting her used to the new set-up to building a good relationship and staying involved with her carer and respecting any regulations associated with her care. If you can keep good lines of communication open between you, you're on the way to creating a good rapport, and by abiding by the rules you'll earn the respect of your child's carer.

Preparing your child

The most important preparation you can give your baby or child is to make planned visits to her childcare provider – even if it's her granny, if you've not left her before – in the run-up to her first full session. Registered providers usually have a suggested routine, but do make it clear if you'd like to make additional visits to what has been planned for your child. It's usual to stay with your child during her first visit; then to leave her, but remain on the premises or nearby on her next visit; and finally to leave her for a full session. You may find, though, that you will be happier to accompany her, then leave her a couple more times, for increasing periods, before making the big break.

Coping in the first few days

How you deal with separating from your baby or child will play a big part in how easily she accepts the separation. Try not to appear upset or cry in front of her, however emotional you may feel, as this is likely to make her panic. Give her a quick kiss and a hug, and a cheery 'Bye bye, see you later', before walking away without hesitation. It will probably feel like the least natural thing you have ever done, but it really is best for both you and your child if you can leave in as low-key a manner as possible – and she is far more likely to be distracted happily if there is no drama to the separation. The more you prolong the agony, the more difficult it will be for both of you, and what should at worst be a few tricky moments can quickly turn into a scene of heart-wrenching torture!

When staff assure you that your child will be fine after a few minutes, believe them. If necessary, phone them to check that she has settled, then once again later in the day – but don't badger staff by calling them every hour or so, as the bond of trust will be broken and you will probably be interrupting an enjoyable period of interactivity between your child and her carer. Rest assured that staff will call you if any emergency arises, and that they are highly experienced with coping with these early separations, both from a parent's and child's point of view. At first, you may feel that the whole process is positively barbaric – but the facts are that separation is necessary, and that your baby or child is highly likely to have recovered completely within a few minutes of your leaving her. Once you have completed the first week of childcare, you are almost certain to begin to feel much more positive about the whole arrangement.

Establishing a rapport

At a nursery where a key worker scheme operates, your child's key worker will be your main point of contact, but it's also worth getting to know the manageress so that you can approach her with any difficulties that can't be resolved between you. Work at building a relationship with the other staff, too, as they will all have a hand in your child's care, and you'll need to liaise and interact with them when your child's key worker is away. It's as much in your child's interest as your own that you establish these bonds, as the more people who recognise you and know whose mum you are, the more channels of communication will be open to you.

In a nursery or playgroup setting, it's usual to make an appointment to speak with your child's key worker or playleader if there is anything you need to discuss in detail. Brief updates can be exchanged at dropping-off or picking-up times, but these aren't good occasions for lengthy conversations as, along with mealtimes, they are the busiest times of the day with many children to organise and parents to greet. Your child's daily record book is also a good tool for communicating with nursery staff, especially if there is an issue that you would like to be 'on the record'. Here you can put in writing any concerns you may have, as well as conveying other information you think may be useful to your child's carers.

The relationship between a parent and her childminder is often much less formal than with nursery or playgroup staff. Because she is in her home environment, a childminder is more likely to be relaxed and self-assured – and because she will be caring for six children at most, her relationship with both you and your child can be more intimate. You may want her to keep a daily diary for your child just so that you do have a device for recording any important conversations between you, but the chances are you'll have more time for a brief conversation at the end of each day without having had to make an appointment, than you would do at a nursery or playgroup.

Respecting boundaries

Whilst the relationship with your child's key worker or playleader will always be on a formal footing, there's usually room for some personal conversation and humour – and your child's antics are likely to provide a good basis for the latter! Although you are paying for the services of your child's playleader or key worker, the primary concern for both of you should be your child's welfare, so it will help the relationship between you enormously if you can place yourself on an equal footing rather than seeing her as an employee and yourself as an employer. Ask her a little about herself, and share some details about yourself too. It's equally important to bear in mind, though, that this is a professional arrangement and, as such, there will be boundaries on either side that should not be crossed.

One potential stumbling block with childminders is that some parents begin to regard their childminder as a friend rather than as a service provider, and if the relationship becomes too cosy, it can be difficult for either side to air any grievances. You may find, for instance, that you feel bound to put up with niggles that you would have complained about in a more formal setting; from the childminder's point of view, she may feel obliged to waive some of her rules, put up with poor timekeeping or find herself unable to say no to any favours you may ask. Again, placing yourselves on an equal footing and giving her due consideration and respect need not bar you from forming a good bond – on the contrary, it's more likely to facilitate a friendly relationship when you both recognise and respect the boundaries.

Working together

Mutual cooperation is key when it comes to forging a healthy relationship with your child's carer. If, for instance, her key worker, playleader or childminder is encountering difficulties in getting your child to eat well, the problem is most likely to be resolved by working together to find a solution or a compromise. If you are finding toilet training problematic, perhaps your childcarer's greater experience can come into play and you can devise between you an action plan that you can both follow consistently. In other words, the aim should be to join forces with your child's carer. Once your child recognises that you are presenting a united front, she will have less scope for playing you off against each other, and you yourself are less likely to cave in from emotional pressure if you know this means letting her carer down – and, ultimately, your child, too.

Giving and getting feedback

It's very important that both you and your child's carer keep each other posted of any domestic or other changes or behavioural issues that arise concerning your child. If, for instance, the family dynamic is about to change – say, with another baby on the way – or if there is going to be some physical disruption, such as a house move, these big life changes may be reflected in a change in your child's behaviour. Sometimes it can be difficult to see a direct link, but general disruption, both physical and emotional, can have a subtle – or more obvious – knock-on effect. This is not unusual, but should be reported as early as possible to your child's carer so that allowances can be made and strategies for helping your child to cope put in place.

If your child's sleeping pattern has been disrupted – for example, by the onset of night terrors, this could also affect her demeanour and performance the next day, so do warn her carer: unexplained changes in disposition or behaviour could otherwise be attributed wrongly to other factors. Similarly, if your child starts exhibiting uncharacteristic behaviour despite a settled and normal home life, you will need to know about any possible underlying causes. Has she been on the receiving end of mistreatment by another child, for example? Has she been upset by one of her favourite staff members being away? Perhaps she has had a bad reaction to a new food on the menu or her best friend has been off sick for a few days?

Make time to find out as much as possible about what's going on during her days with her carer, so that you can start to piece things together between you.

It's natural at first to want to know every detail of what your child has been up to all day every day, but this just won't be possible. However, you should be able to get reasonable feedback via her daily record or diary, chats with her carer and scheduled lengthier updates where necessary. Don't be afraid to ask for an appointment for a full progress report every now and then, even if you don't have any particular worries or concerns: your child's carer will appreciate your interest and should be more than happy to update you at a time that suits you both.

Exchanging feedback also encompasses ironing out any niggles you or your childminder may have. Awkward though it can seem to have to express your unhappiness with any element of your carer's practice, it's important to air your feelings as soon possible after they arise. Unless you act sooner rather than later, an unacceptable practice will simply continue, and the longer you leave it to say something, the harder it will become. The same applies if your carer is unhappy, so make it clear that you are very willing to listen to any grievances and work together to put things right. You may even decide to introduce a regular mutual appraisal session where one or both of you can discuss any minor issues you may have.

The power of praise

Don't forget to praise your child's carer regularly: it will contribute greatly to her job satisfaction if you show your appreciation, and a happy carer means a happier environment for your child. As with all situations where you are parting with hard-earned cash in return for a service, the impulse is to complain or criticise when things go wrong, but there's often very little drive to make a point of taking notice when things run smoothly. It's not necessary to ply your child's carer with gifts – although a bottle of wine or some flowers at Christmas or the end of each term won't go amiss – but a few well-chosen words or the occasional card (perhaps made by your child) will go a long way towards helping your relationship to flourish.

> *'I was mortified to be asked by my childminder, Jo, about three months into our arrangement, whether or not I was happy with the care she was giving. She said that Tom seemed to enjoy his time with her, but that she wanted to be sure that she was doing OK by me. I was embarrassed to realise that I had completely neglected to give her any feedback: she's a mature lady who clearly knows what she's doing and I'm very happy with her; I just assumed she would know. Now I make a point of passing Tom's cheery little comments about his day back to her when I next see her: the other day he said, "I love Jo-jo – it's like having another granny". Sharing little incidents like this are something I know Jo will treasure, and passing on praise is something that's too easily overlooked.'*
>
> Jan Fisher, 30, mum to Tom, three

Monitoring your under-five's development

Child development is an interaction between a child's inborn abilities and the environment in which she is raised, so if the childcare programme of activities is uninspiring, her enthusiasm for learning and her motivation to progress are likely to diminish. On the other hand, an inspiring setting should help to encourage her in all areas of development. Knowing some of what your child should be achieving at which age and stage will help you to assess whether or not her childcarer is bringing her on developmentally. Each child is different and will progress at his or her own rate, and if you or your carer are worried that your baby or child is not making progress consistent with her age and stage, consult your health visitor or GP, who will be able to make a good assessment.

Here's a rough guide to what to expect and when, plus what sorts of activities a great childcarer (including you!) can provide to help her at each stage. Share it with your childcarer if you think it's appropriate.

By 0–4 months

Your baby will smile and laugh, will recognise her carer(s) approaching, will reach for toys dangling from her cot and will enjoy mimicking facial expressions.

Activities to encourage her include:

- dangling toys in strongly contrasting colours (e.g. black and white) near her face so that she can see them close up and make a grab if she wants to.

- pulling lots of faces for her to copy: try making an 'o' with your mouth or looking surprised, and watch and wait for her to copy before adopting the next expression.
- referring to yourself by name as often as you use her name: say, 'Here comes Mummy! Here I am now!' or 'Are you smiling at Mummy?'

By 4–6 months

Your baby may push herself up from lying on her tummy to supporting herself on her forearms to get a better all-round view. She may also roll over – from front to back first, then later back to front – and sit up with support.

Activities to encourage her include:

- dangling interesting toys just above her so that they catch her eye from a prone lying position.
- calling or singing to her from a little way above her head.
- rattling a toy to the side of her that she usually prefers to roll towards.
- propping her up on the floor (so she can't fall from a height) with cushions all around her to keep her upright; passing her toys to play with; reading and singing to her and pointing out things for her to focus on.

By 6–9 months

Your baby may sit unsupported, crawl, 'walk' holding your hands, babble and try to feed herself finger foods.

Activities to encourage her include:

- placing interesting objects just out of her reach so that she has an incentive to stretch or propel herself forwards by bottom shuffling, commando-style crawling (where she drags herself along by her forearms) or hands-and-knees crawling.
- holding a toy or hand out near to her when she's crawling to encourage her to reach up with one hand. This is the first step towards 'cruising', where she will use furniture as a support whilst 'walking' around the room.
- babbling back to her and making easy, repetitive sounds for her to copy: 'bababa', 'dadada' and so on. (Sadly, 'mamama' is not as easy for a beginner to enunciate as these others, but don't worry, it'll come later!)
- providing a range of finger foods that are easy to pick up: not slippery pasta, but carrot and cucumber sticks (also great for teething babies to gnaw on straight from the fridge), cheese cubes, breadsticks, sugar-free rusks and so on.
- attaching a toy to her highchair playtray by a short piece of ribbon so she can practise grasping it and dropping it, then pulling it back up by the ribbon. (This way you won't have to keep on picking it up for her!)
- letting her 'stand' supported and make stepping movements in your lap.

By 9–12 months
Your baby may pull herself up to standing and 'cruise' around the room, holding on to furniture for support; she may crawl up and over objects.

Activities to encourage her include:

- placing toys within her eyeline at standing height so that she's keen to get to her feet and examine them.
- offering your hand for support if she seems to be struggling to get to her feet.
- putting a few soft 'obstacles' in her way, then holding a favourite toy at the other end so that she tackles the obstacles to get to it.
- providing a secure soft-play area.
- providing a baby door bouncer for her to use in short bursts (no longer than 20 minutes at a time) to strengthen her legs, encourage a sense of independence and give her the perspective of being upright.

By 12–18 months
Your baby may walk independently (although this can happen any time from nine to 18 months, occasionally later), say a few words and feed herself with a spoon.

Activities to encourage her include:

- kneeling a few short steps away from her with outstretched arms and encouraging her to propel herself forwards.

- taking her for short walks on baby reins once she has found her feet fairly confidently (with properly fitted shoes if you're outdoors).
- really listening to the words she's trying to formulate and looking for visual clues to help you make sense of what she's saying.
- repeating simple words and phrases often, especially when she is showing an interest in something: 'There's the cat. There's the cat again. Let's stroke the cat.' Or 'Where's Ellie's book? Is this Ellie's book? Let's read Ellie's book together.'
- using her name often: 'Is Ellie hungry? Is Ellie thirsty? Good girl, Ellie. That's great, Ellie.'
- allowing her to eat with a spoon, even if not much food actually reaches her mouth!
- offering a variety of several spoonable foods you know she enjoys at each meal to tempt her into practising more and more.
- playing coordination action games, such as 'The wheels on the bus' or 'If you're happy and you know it touch your mouth; if you're happy and you know it touch your knees; touch your mouth, touch your knees, touch your head, touch your nose' and so on.

By 18–24 months
Your toddler may make two- or three-word sentences; become potty-trained (although night-time training may come later); run and jump.

Activities to encourage her include:

- reading, reading and more reading to help her start to understand full sentences.
- chatting as much as possible and, instead of correcting her grammar, simply repeating what she says in the correct form. For example: 'I didded it!' 'You *did* it, did you?' or 'My toy broked!' 'Your toy *broke*? What a shame!'
- watching for signs that your child needs the loo so that accidents can be prevented where possible, thus avoiding the feelings of failure that sometimes plague toddlers. (This is often easier for a childminder or parent/friend carer than nursery staff because of the more intensive care.)
- making frequent trips to the loo whether the signs are there or not: toddlers are often quite willing to sit on the potty at regular times – say, soon after a meal – especially if they are permitted to play or read whilst sitting there. Even if nothing is produced at first, a routine can often be established with time and persistence.
- encouraging outdoor play, including ball games, obstacle races, access to low climbing apparatus and so on.

By 2–3 years

Your child may be formulating full sentences; able to hold a pencil and produce rudimentary drawings involving circles, lines and crosses; produce very early letter shapes;

start being able to count in sequence; build a tower of up to 10 bricks.

Activities to encourage her include:

- chatting to her often – and remembering always to allow sufficient time for her full reply (and not to anticipate or finish off sentences for her).
- reading books with increasing amounts of text per page, as long as they hold her interest – and encouraging her to predict what might happen next.
- providing her with a pencil and paper so that she can scribble and experiment with forming shapes.
- showing her how to form her own name: this often provides the incentive for a child to begin trying to write.
- writing simple words in dotted outlines for her to 'trace'.
- praising all her efforts at speaking, writing and drawing.
- playing counting games and singing counting rhymes and songs whenever appropriate.
- challenging her to build the tallest tower of bricks she can, then encouraging her to knock them all down and start again.

By 4–5 years

Your child's coordination continues to strengthen, and by the time she is five, her balance will be almost as good as yours. Some time between the ages of four and five she will stand on tiptoes, hop on one foot, master the ability to turn somersaults and perhaps even skip with a rope. She'll become more independent when attempting tasks such as brushing her teeth and dressing herself. Her hand skills, drawing, letter formation and number skills will be improving, as will her ability to cut and paste and paint with a paintbrush. She will soon be able to formulate sentences of up to eight words at a time.

Activities to encourage her include:

- playing balancing games, such as musical statues or low-beam walking.
- increasing opportunities for physical play, including obstacles courses and more challenging climbing apparatus.
- encouraging her to try riding a bike (probably with stabilisers at first).
- giving her more freedom to handle her own self-care (although teeth should always be checked after brushing until about age seven because most children lack the necessary dexterity until then).
- inspiring her with ideas for new drawings, collages, patterns and other art and craft activities, and providing her with a variety of materials.
- setting her up for supervised painting sessions.
- reading to her frequently and encouraging her to read herself – even everyday things, such as road signs and street names.

- talking to her and finding out her ideas about things – remembering to listen closely and reflect back to her what she's told you, for example:

  Your child: 'I really like playing mummies and babies, especially when I'm the mummy.'
  You: 'I can see why you enjoy playing mummies and babies: you make a very good mummy to your toys.'

Making a part-time school nursery place work for you

If you are able to take up a state school nursery place at the school you're hoping your child will attend, there will be several advantages: your child will meet and interact with children who will start full-time school with her later on; you will have an opportunity to get to know the school and staff in advance (also allowing you to apply elsewhere, should you feel dissatisfied with what you see); and you will save a great deal of money on other types of childcare.

The downside, especially for working parents, is that children attend for only a morning or afternoon session a day, five days a week. In some instances, you may not have a choice over whether your child's placement is in the mornings or afternoons, although in others you might; in any case, it can be tricky to juggle working hours and other commitments.

For many parents, the answer is to employ a childminder or enlist the help of a parent or friend to fill in when the child is not at nursery, and take her or bring her home when she is. For others, renegotiating or reducing working hours or switching to part-homeworking is the most practical answer.

In some instances, it simply won't be possible to take up the free nursery place because work or other commitments cannot be rescheduled and supplementary childcare is not a practical solution.

What mums say about part-time carers

'Without Mum and Dad, I just don't know how we would have managed. We rely on my salary as much as my husband's, so I had to return to my nursing job when Zach was a year old, almost two years ago. I managed to renegotiate my hours so that I just work in daytime clinics now rather than doing shifts, and Mum and Dad's help has meant that Zach's been able to go to the nursery attached to our local primary school in the afternoons. Mum takes him in and Dad collects him and looks after him while Mum goes to her part-time job locally. I think it's great that Zach has so much time with his grandad – and Dad is becoming a "new man" in his sixties! Mum says he didn't used to change my or my brother's nappies or make us any meals, but now he's doing the lot!'

Zoe, 29, mum to Zach, almost three

'I was lucky enough to find Cassie, a really excellent childminder, through our local primary school: my neighbour's little boy is in the reception class there,

and he used to go to her from when he was newborn until he started school, so Cassie's used to the nursery hours and is already familiar with the staff and the general set-up. It's really good to know that my daughter, Molly, is being cared for by someone who has links with the school already – in a way it makes me feel as if Cassie's an extension of the school. I drop Molly off at 8 a.m. before going on to my job as an aerobics instructor at the local leisure centre, which I love. I pick her up again at 3 p.m. when I finish. Meanwhile, Cassie takes Molly to nursery and picks her up again. Molly is very happy with the arrangement, even though she only met Cassie a few weeks before she started at the nursery. All in all, I'm relieved that I don't have to feel guilty about going to work.'

Allison, 32, mum to Molly, two and a half

What if you suspect lazy or negligent care?

One of the most worrying aspects of childcare for many parents is the feeling of not knowing what's going on 'behind closed doors'. There have been very public exposés in recent times about poorly run nurseries and abusive nannies and other minders, and these have done nothing to promote parents' confidence in allowing other people to look after their precious children. Thankfully, these incidents are newsworthy only because of their rarity. All professions, especially the caring ones, do inevitably attract some undesirables, but because all childcare is now subject to stringent monitoring and regulation, there is less margin for negligent or abusive practice.

One way of checking that the care your child is receiving is of a consistently high standard is to drop in occasionally, unannounced, at different times of the day. Seeing that your child is happily occupied, sleeping peacefully or enjoying some outdoor fun should reassure you. If you are unhappy with what you find – or if you have other cause for concern (see below) – there are steps you can take to get the problem rectified or to change your childcare arrangements (see page 141).

Spotting the signs of inferior care

There are some telltale signs that the care your child is receiving may not be up to standard, and some of these can even be spotted in babies. It's important to be on the alert for signs of neglect or abuse; however, the following signs don't necessarily mean that any abusive or negligent behaviour is going on: it could just be that something is unsettling your child. Either way, if your child's carer is confident in her skills and the standard of care she is providing, she will be happy for you to investigate and to suggest some changes.

Signs to watch for in a baby include:

- disrupted feeding or sleeping patterns.
- crying more than usual.
- a sudden reversion to clingy or distressed behaviour in a formerly settled baby when you try to leave her (although this behaviour is common at around seven to nine months).
- more withdrawn behaviour than usual.

- being more easily startled by loud noises or sudden movements.
- unexplained or unsubstantiated marking or injury to the body.

In a toddler or older child, look and listen for:

- clingy, withdrawn, passive or lethargic behaviour in a previously energetic, confident child.
- over-extrovert or attention-seeking behaviour in a previously reticent child.
- frequent claims of feeling unwell on daycare days.
- excessive crying or apparent unhappiness.
- disruptions to normal routines.
- not wanting to go to bed.
- negative comments about her minder.
- getting excessively upset or nervous when you tell her off.
- general out-of-character behaviour.
- unexplained or unsubstantiated marking or injury to the body.

'Additionally, if your child reports that her carer insists on spending time alone with her, out of sight of others, treats her differently in any way from other children under her care, asks her to keep secrets of any sort or touches her in any way that could be construed as inappropriate, the situation certainly merits close and immediate investigation,' warns chartered educational psychologist Dr Richard Woolfson.

Making a complaint

The first port of call – unless, of course, you have reason to suspect genuine neglect or abuse – should usually be the childcare provider: it will be far easier for everyone concerned, and less disruptive for your child, if you can resolve matters between you. In a nursery, explore the possibility of a change of key worker, and find out if there is another child or group of children that is making your child feel uncomfortable or unhappy. If your child is unhappy with her childminder, nanny or au pair, talking to her in detail about how she is responding to your child's needs and asking about any difficulties between them may highlight areas for change.

If you are unable to resolve any problems between you, or if you believe that your child's carer has acted inappropriately or irresponsibly, you are entitled to make an official complaint to the following bodies:

- In England: the Office for Standards in Education (Ofsted): 0845 601 4772.
- In Wales: the Care Standards Inspectorate for Wales (CSIW): 029 2047 8600.
- In Scotland: the Care Commission: 01382 207100.
- In Northern Ireland: the Northern Ireland Child Minding Association: 028 9181 1015.

If you suspect abuse

If you have any reason to suspect abuse or if you have any concerns about the safety of any child under the care of your chosen provider, it's always in the best interests of the child to follow your instincts. A good starting point is the National Society for the Prevention of Cruelty to Children (NSPCC): 0808 800 5000 (24 hours) or textphone: 0800 056 0566. Otherwise, contact the police or social services.

Making a change

Sometimes, a child may simply not take to her childminder or other carer – or it could be that the type of care you have chosen for her doesn't suit her personality or stage of development. In this case – as well as in cases of substandard or neglectful care – you'll have to make a change. 'It's not something, however, that should be rushed into unless you are really sure that your child is not going to adjust,' says Dr Woolfson. 'Remember that children take time to settle – often up to eight weeks; after that adjustment period, the placement may prove to be very fruitful and satisfactory, despite what might have seemed a troubled start.'

If there are no signs of progress after a period of around eight weeks, it may be that your child is simply not ready for childcare. If, however, you feel intuitively that it's the setting that is at fault rather than childcare itself, the best thing is to remove your child as soon as you can, even if this means paying for childcare you don't actually use whilst the agreed notice period elapses. 'If you don't act promptly, and your child is left in an unsuitable placement for too long, she will fail to thrive psychologically or make as much developmental progress as expected,' Dr Woolfson points out. 'Some children may even begin to regress – that is, to behave like a younger child again. In the short term, these effects will quickly reverse once she moves to a more fulfilling placement, but the emotional impact of an unsuitable placement becomes more enduring the longer it goes on.'

Refer back to your previous shortlist of possible carers and see how well each would fit in with your child's needs as well as your working hours. Perhaps you could negotiate with your partner to share your child's care by changing his working hours? Maybe you could swap to a combination of childcare: for example, childminder plus parent/friend; or free nursery place plus childminder (see page 143).

Whether or not much time has elapsed, it's sensible to revisit your next choice of childcare provider: it could be that changes have happened since your last visit that you or your child won't be happy with. There's no need necessarily to be quite as rigorous in your interviewing as the first time around, but do make sure you both get a proper feel for the place and the main carer(s) again before coming to a decision.

If your child hasn't settled, it may be that she is just not ready to go to childcare provision yet – and this may be confirmed if she fails to settle in with a second or subsequent carer. In this case, see what you can do to adapt your working hours, change your role, juggle your commitments and your partner's, or even take an unpaid break from work. It might seem a huge sacrifice now, but will probably prove to be, in the end, a relatively minor glitch in your family's life, and it may be only a matter of weeks before you feel your child is ready to try again.

Combining types of childcare

For some families, a combination of different types of childcare provision works out best for everyone. Some parents choose to ring the changes by taking up a private nursery place two days a week, then swapping to a childminder, relative or friend for the remainder, feeling that this will give their child a more rounded experience of pre-school care as well as familiarising her with a variety of different activities and people. For others it's a matter of practicality, either because the cost of full-time formal childcare is prohibitive or because they can't juggle their working hours to fit around one type of childcare alone.

If your child does attend a state nursery for the two years leading up to her full-time school place, you will have to make other arrangements for her during the 14 weeks of the year when there is no free provision. In this case it's sensible to have the services of a childminder, relative or friend lined up in advance to cover these holiday periods.

The key thing to bear in mind is that your child still needs as much consistency of care as you can arrange.

So if, for instance, she is following a particular toilet-training programme at her state nursery, you should brief her holiday-cover carers to follow the same regime if possible. Similarly, if she is at a nursery where naps happen at set times of day, ask other carers to follow the same pattern if this is practical. Share information between your child's carers as to how she is getting on, emotionally and developmentally, and keep all people involved in her care up to date with any big changes or upheavals that could potentially upset or otherwise affect her.

> *'My employer agreed quite readily to me working mornings from home, then coming into the office in the afternoons so that Jonathon could take up his free nursery place. But when it came to working full time from home during school holidays, we both knew it would never work out. A friend had recently hired a part-time nanny, so I agreed with my boss that I'd work two and a half days a week in the office and the rest from home – and I "borrowed" her nanny to cover for me, just for the holidays. The rest of my work was done from home – but I have to admit that I was cramming some of it into evenings and weekends when my partner was around because Jonathon was, quite understandably, too demanding to allow me to work for hours on end. Still, it was better to put up with this arrangement for a few weeks at a time than to have to give up my job.'*
>
> Suzi, 29, mum to Jonathon, three

Chapter 7

Drawing up a contract – and other legalities

When you are acting as employer to your childcare provider – when you hire a nanny, childminder or au pair, that is – the best footing for the relationship is to agree between you a workable contract. With a nanny, a document similar to a contract, known as Particulars of Employment, is a legal requirement. This is an outline of the basic job description and terms and conditions, all of which can be incorporated into a contract of your own design. When you employ a childminder, she will usually produce a contract for you both to complete (often one drawn up by the National Childminding Association).

Drawing up a contract doesn't give you free rein to lay down the law about what you will and won't tolerate; nor is this a document that is solely about what your carer will or won't do for you. It is a contract of employment, which means that there will be terms to be agreed on both sides.

You could get a solicitor to draw up a contract for you, but this will incur an expense that is, frankly, usually unnecessary in these circumstances. Over the next few pages is a sample contract for families to use for nannies, derived from one drawn up by childcare recruitment consultants Nannyjob. You can copy and paste the document from their website (www.nannyjob.co.uk), or use the revised and updated version below.

Model contract of employment for nannies

(Where necessary, please delete as appropriate.)

Dated: ....

BETWEEN

(1) ('the Employer') ....

(2) ('the Nanny') ....

Our agreement with you:

IT IS AGREED that the Employer will employ the Nanny on the following terms and conditions:

1. Terms of Employment

1.1 The Nanny is employed to work at the Employer's home or such other place(s) as the Employer may reasonably require from time to time. The employment commenced on .... and shall not be continuous with any previous period of employment.

1.2 The Nanny's duties shall be:

(a) caring for children who names and ages are: ....

(b) babysitting at times agreed in advance.

The Nanny will be required to undertake additional duties as the Employer may require from time to time.

1.3 The Nanny shall normally work the following days:
....

1.4 Normal Working Hours shall be agreed by the Employer and Nanny in advance, but shall generally be: ....

1.5 The Nanny shall be entitled to rest periods in accordance with the Working Time Regulations 1998 (and any regulations amending the same).

1.6 Unless prevented by illness or injury the Nanny shall:

   (a) devote the whole of her time, attention and ability, both during normal Working Hours and during such other reasonable additional hours as may be agreed between the Employer and Nanny, for the performance of her duties for the employer;
   (b) follow all lawful instructions of the Employer;
   (c) not perform any paid or unpaid work for any third party without the prior written consent of the Employer.

2. Remuneration

2.1 The Nanny's gross salary will be £........... per (week/month). The salary shall be reviewed (once/twice) a year on .... but any increase in salary shall be at the total discretion of the Employer.

2.2 The salary shall be payable in arrears on the last working day in each (week/month) by a cheque or a standing order payment direct to the Nanny's bank, as agreed by the parties. The Employer shall ensure that the Nanny is given a payslip on the date of payment detailing gross payment, deductions and net payment.

2.3 The Nanny shall receive the following benefits:

   (a) Accommodation
   The Employer provides the following accommodation:
   ....

(b) Meals
The Employer provides the following meals:
....

(c) Use of car
The Employer (does/does not) provide the use of a car.

(d) Pension
The Employer (does/does not) provide pension contributions.

(e) Private Health Scheme
The Employer does/does not provide private health insurance.

2.4 The Nanny shall be reimbursed by the Employer for all reasonable expenses incurred by her in the performance of her duties under this contract, provided that the expenses are incurred with the approval of the Employer and provided the Nanny produces such evidence of expenditure as the Employer may reasonably require. Petrol costs will be reimbursed at the rate recommended by the Automobile Association if the Nanny uses her own car during performance of her duties.

2.5 The Nanny agrees that the employer shall be entitled to deduct from any amount payable to the Nanny under this contract:

(a) any deductions required by law (including PAYE income tax and National Insurance Contributions);
(b) any monies owed by her to the Employer by way of reimbursement.

2.6 The Employer shall be responsible for accounting to the Inland Revenue for Income Tax and the Employer's and the Nanny's National Insurance Contributions.

3. Holidays

3.1 The holiday year will start on ....
....

3.2 In each holiday year the Nanny's holiday entitlement is 20 days* (including the usual public and bank holidays).

3.3 Holiday pay will be made at the Nanny's normal rate of remuneration. One day's holiday pay is calculated as the Nanny's annual salary divided by the number of working days per year.

3.4 The Nanny will not be allowed to carry holiday forward from one leave year to the next or (subject to clause 3.7) receive payment in lieu of any untaken holiday entitlement, and the Nanny shall ensure that she takes such entitlement within the holiday year.

3.5 The Nanny shall give the Employer not less than ..... weeks' notice of an intention to take a holiday. If the holiday period requested is not convenient to the Employer, the Employer shall agree an alternative period that is convenient to both parties. The Nanny will not be allowed to take more than 10 working days' holiday at any one time. There is no entitlement to take unpaid holidays. (Please note that this clause must not be used if it effectively deprives the Nanny of taking her holiday in the holiday year.)

3.6 Where the Nanny is working out any notice following either party giving notice to terminate this contract, the Nanny may be required to take any unused holiday during that notice period.

3.7 Holiday entitlement for any part of the year worked will be calculated on a pro rata basis at the rate of days per calendar month worked.

3.8 On the termination of her employment, the Nanny will be paid any holiday entitlement accrued but not taken. If the Nanny has taken more days' holiday than her accrued entitlement, the Employer will make the appropriate deduction from the Nanny's final salary payment (calculated in accordance with clause 4.3).

3.9 If the Nanny is required to work on a bank holiday or other public holiday, the Nanny will be given a day off in lieu on a date to be agreed by the Employer.

4. Sickness & Sick Pay

4.1 If the Nanny is unable to attend work because of sickness or injury, she shall notify the Employer either in person or by telephone (as appropriate) by 8.30 a.m. on the first day of absence. If the Nanny is absent for more than one day, she will keep the Employer regularly informed of the expected duration of her absence.

4.2 The Nanny will provide the Employer with such evidence of her sickness or injury and the cause of it as the Employer may reasonably require, and if the Nanny is absent for more than seven days (including weekends), she will provide the Employer with a medical certificate for each subsequent week of sickness absence.

4.3 The Nanny shall be entitled to receive Statutory Sick Pay (SSP) in accordance with the government SSP scheme during periods of sickness absence as follows:

(a) full pay for the first .... days/weeks' sick leave;
(b) half pay for ... days/weeks;
(c) thereafter Statutory Sick Pay in accordance with the government's SSP scheme.

4.4 The Employer shall be entitled to require the Nanny to undergo examinations by a medical practitioner appointed by the Employer, and the Nanny shall sign the necessary consent form to authorise the medical practitioner to disclose to the Employer the results of the examination, and discuss with the Employer any matters arising from the examination that might impair the Nanny's ability to properly discharge her duties.

4.5 If the Nanny takes sick leave because of injuries caused to her by a third party, and the Nanny recovers damages from the third party for her injuries, the damages recovered shall include all payments made to the Nanny by the Employer during the sick leave, and all payments recovered shall then be paid to the Employer as soon as possible.

5. Confidentiality

5.1 The Nanny shall not during her employment with the Employer, or at any time thereafter (otherwise than in the proper course of her duties or as is required by law) without the prior written approval of the Employer, use, divulge or disclose any information relating directly or indirectly to the personal or business affairs of the Employer or any member of the Employer's family.

5.2 At the termination of her employment the Nanny will ensure that all documentation relating to the children and other members of the Employer's family is immediately returned to the Employer.

6. Termination

6.1 If either party wishes to terminate this contract, the notice to be given in writing shall be as follows:

(a) during the first four weeks of employment ('the Probationary Period'), not less than one week's notice.
(b) from the first day of the fifth week of service until the last day of the fourth year of service, not less than four weeks' notice.
(c) thereafter, the notice period shall increase by one week for each completed year of service (e.g. five weeks' notice for five complete years' service, six weeks' notice for six complete years' service) up to a maximum of 12 weeks' notice for 12 complete years' service or more.

6.2 The Nanny's employment under this contract may be terminated by the Employer at any time immediately and without any notice or payment in lieu of notice if the Nanny:

(a) is guilty of gross misconduct or serious and persistent breaches of the terms of this contract, or
(b) is convicted of any criminal offence involving dishonesty, violence, causing death or personal injury, or damaging property.

6.3 Misconduct that may be deemed gross misconduct includes, but is not limited to, theft, drunkenness, illegal drug-taking, child abuse and violent or threatening behaviour (be it verbal or physical).

7. Disciplinary & Capability Procedure

7.1 Reasons that might give rise to the need for measures under the Disciplinary & Capability Procedure include the following:

(a) causing a disruptive influence in the household;
(b) job incompetence;
(c) unsatisfactory standard of dress or appearance;
(d) conduct inside or outside Normal Working Hours prejudicial to the interests or reputation of the Employer;
(e) unreliability in time-keeping or attendance;
(f) failure to comply with instructions and procedures;
(g) loss of driving licence;
(h) breach of confidentiality.

This list is not exhaustive and may also include any other reason that the Employer reasonably considers may qualify as misconduct or lack of capability.

7.2 The Employer shall have the right to suspend the Nanny from her duties on full pay or such terms and conditions as the Employer shall determine for the purpose of conducting an investigation in relation to any allegation of misconduct in advance of any disciplinary hearing.

7.3 If disciplinary procedures are instigated, the Nanny will be informed of the complaint against her in advance of a disciplinary hearing taking place. The Nanny will have the right to appeal against any disciplinary action taken against her.

7.4 In the event of the Employer needing to take disciplinary action the procedure shall, save in cases involving gross misconduct, be:

first:	verbal warning
second:	written warning
third:	dismissal

8. Grievance Procedure

8.1 If the Nanny has any reasonable grievance relating to her employment, the matter should be raised with the Employer. The Nanny should raise the grievance informally in the first instance, but if the matter is not resolved, the matter should be raised in writing with the Employer. The Employer and the Nanny agree to take all such reasonable steps as are necessary to resolve such grievances.**

9. General

9.1 This contract shall be construed in accordance with and governed by the laws of England and Wales/Scotland/Northern Ireland, and the parties submit to the exclusive jurisdiction of the Courts of England and Wales/Scotland/Northern Ireland.

9.2 Any reference in this contract to any statutory provision shall be deemed to include a reference to any statutory modification or re-enactment of it and shall also include reference to all statutory instruments and orders made pursuant to any such statutory provision.

9.3 Words in the singular shall include the plural and vice versa, and references to any gender shall include the other, and a reference to a person shall include a reference to any Company as well as any legal or natural person.

9.4 This contract replaces any previous particulars of employment issued to the Nanny and constitutes the whole agreement between the parties.

9.5 The Employer reserves the right to make reasonable changes to any of the Nanny's terms and conditions of employment. The Nanny will be given not less than one month's written notice of any significant changes relating to the Nanny's employment.

SIGNED by the Employer ....

DATED ....

SIGNED by the Nanny ....

DATED ....

* The current statutory minimum paid holiday for employees is 20 days, including eight days' bank holiday. You may offer more than this if you wish. Please note that the statutory minimum is rising to 24 days from 1 October 2007, and to 28 days from 1 October 2008.

If your Nanny's holiday year commences on a day other than 1 October, you will be obliged to provide extra days holiday pro rata for the remainder of your Nanny's holiday year.

For ease of calculation, you may note how much paid holiday your Nanny is entitled to by using the table below. For example, a Nanny whose holiday year runs from 1 January will be entitled to 4.2 weeks' paid holiday (i.e. 21 days' paid holiday) for 2007.

Leave year start	**2006–7**	**2007–8**	**2008–9**
1 November	4.07 weeks	4.87 weeks	5.6 weeks
1 December	4.13 weeks	4.93 weeks	
	2007	**2008**	**2009**
1 January	4.2 weeks	5 weeks	5.6 weeks
	2007–8	**2008–9**	**2009–10**
1 February	4.27 weeks	5.07 weeks	
1 March	4.33 weeks	5.13 weeks	
1 April	4.4 weeks	5.2 weeks	
1 May	4.47 weeks	5.27 weeks	
1 June	4.53 weeks	5.33 weeks	5.6 weeks
1 July	4.6 weeks	5.4 weeks	
1 August	4.67 weeks	5.47 weeks	

	2007–8	2008–9	2009–10
1 September	4.73 weeks	5.53 weeks	
1 October	4.8 weeks	5.6 weeks	

** Please note that if an employee raises a grievance, you must comply with the statutory grievance procedures. Requirements under the procedures include inviting the employee to attend a grievance meeting, informing the employee of his or her right to be accompanied, providing a decision in writing, and giving the employee an opportunity to appeal against any decision made.

Au pair contracts

If the arrangement between you and your au pair is to be an employment relationship rather than, say, a voluntary relationship, it would be wise to have a contract similar in content to the nanny contract. It should certainly include the points below, and as an au pair would have the same access to personal information as a nanny, it might be worth including a confidentiality clause too.

- length of employment period
- notice period on either side
- working hours
- duties
- additional babysitting requirements
- remuneration
- complementary benefits (use of car, telephone, etc.) plus restrictions on the use of these
- house rules (regarding smoking/alcohol/boyfriends or girlfriends, etc.)
- holiday entitlement and days off.

Before you hire an au pair

There are a few legal criteria your au pair must meet before your employment arrangement becomes legal.

1. An au pair is a single person aged from 17 to 27 who comes to the UK from an EEA (European Economic Area) country to study English, and lives for up to two years with an English-speaking family.
2. An au pair must be a national of one of the following countries: Andorra, Bosnia-Herzegovina, Bulgaria, Croatia, Cyprus, Czech Republic, Estonia, Faroe Islands, Greenland, Hungary, Latvia, Liechtenstein, Lithuania, Macedonia, Malta, Monaco, Poland, Romania, San Marino, Slovak Republic, Slovenia, Switzerland and Turkey.

   In addition, nationals of Bosnia-Herzegovina, Bulgaria, Croatia, Macedonia, Romania and Turkey must obtain a visa from their designated British Embassy or Consulate before travelling to the United Kingdom.
3. An au pair must be unmarried, without dependants and not intending to stay in the UK for longer than two years as an au pair. She/he must declare her/his intention to leave the UK on completion of her/his stay as an au pair.
4. If your au pair has stayed in the UK for longer than six months, she/he will normally be required to register with the police, and this requirement will be stamped in her/his passport.

Chapter 8

Frequently asked questions

However well you have researched and chosen childcare, there can be few parents who have no qualms or doubts at all about their choices, or about the impact childcare as a whole may have on their life. Here are some of the most common concerns parents have, especially at the start of any new childcare arrangement.

Your baby or child

Q How can I be sure my child will be happy?

A Once you have conducted as thorough an interview as possible with your child's main carer, reassured yourself that all certificates and registration documents are up to date and legitimate and have settled your child in to your satisfaction, you will, to a certain extent, have to trust your own instincts. Bear in mind, also, that if your baby or child comes away from his carer from time to time a bit upset or generally grumpy, there's no saying that he wouldn't have been in precisely the same mood in your care: no person is happy all the time, and children are no different from adults in this regard.

If your baby seems generally settled, is continuing to gain weight, sleep well and socialise as he did before, and is developing as you would hope and expect, you have no reason to suspect that he is anything other than content with the arrangement. If, on the other hand, he is still very reluctant to allow you to leave him after a reasonable settling-in period, and he's inconsolable once you have gone; or if your child is desperate to go home as soon as you arrive to collect him or distressed at the prospect of ever returning, it's safe to assume that he is not benefiting from the arrangement and that you must either delay childcare or find an alternative placement.

Other ways of increasing his happiness might include:

- letting his carer know his favourite songs, rhymes, types of toy, foods and games.
- packing one of his favourite toys to take with him (but nothing so special that, if it were lost or broken, he would be bereft).
- arriving in good time to collect him so that he doesn't feel abandoned.
- building a good relationship with his carer yourself so that he can see she is someone you trust and like.
- letting him take a piece of your clothing (cardigan, scarf or handkerchief) that bears your own special scent and may comfort him.
- not intervening too young to wean him off his comforters (bottle, dummy, special blanket, etc.).
- not pressurising him into mastering other skills so that he 'keeps up' with other children or with what the nursery or childminder would prefer.

- listening to him if he does have a grievance – or, in the case of a young baby, being alert to any negative changes in his routine or behaviour.

Q How much does my baby understand about what's happening?

A You may worry that your young baby will feel terribly torn away from all that is familiar to him without any idea as to why, but what is important to bear in mind is that a baby's immediate priorities are that he is clean, warm, fed and has plenty of cuddles. Yes, he will recognise your own particular voice and smell, but he will survive quite happily without you whilst he is at a very young age, and is unlikely to miss you terribly.

If your baby is at the clingy stage, which typically begins at around seven to nine months, he is likely to understand a little more of what is going on, but he will probably react in the same way as when, for instance, you leave him in his cot to go and fetch his bottle: all he knows is that you have disappeared from sight – and, as far as he understands it, once you have disappeared you may not return. Don't worry too much about this: babies usually settle within minutes of separation as long as they are distracted and have another pair of welcoming arms to comfort them. It's when your baby can still see you but can't reach you that he is likely to seem most upset. You may also find it encouraging to understand that your baby's realisation that you still exist somewhere, even though he can no longer see you, is an important part of his cognitive development.

During this clingy phase may not be the best period to start childcare for the first time, but if you have no alternative, be reassured that it is not so much that you are leaving him with someone else that is upsetting him as the idea that you may not be coming back. As time goes on, he will grow used to the fact that you always do come back for him and, thankfully, this period of anxiety is usually fairly short-lived.

Although another bout of separation anxiety commonly occurs at around 18 months of age, your older baby or toddler may cope more easily with being left, simply because he does understand a little more about where he is and why. Research has shown that even much younger babies understand a lot of what is being said to them far before they are able to articulate anything themselves. By introducing rituals, such as waving goodbye whilst saying 'See you later', and by ensuring that you turn up on time to collect him, you will help him to learn that he is perfectly safe and able to enjoy himself whilst you are away because he knows that you will be coming back. You could even practise saying 'goodbye' to your baby at home, when you have the support of your partner or a favourite relative or friend: wave bye-bye and go out of the door, saying you'll soon be back, then pop your head around the door a few moments later, calling 'hello'. Increase the length of time between leaving the room and coming back, to include a quick trip to the shops, and your baby will eventually begin to understand that 'goodbye' is not the same as 'goodbye forever'!

Q Will my child be emotionally damaged by being separated from me?

A It goes without saying that if a childcare setting cannot meet a child's emotional and developmental needs for attention, stimulation and safety, then it could be psychologically damaging – but separation from you *per se* will not harm your child, as long as you do your research so that you feel as confident as possible that you have chosen the right arrangement. As we have seen in previous chapters, some children thrive better within a home environment, whilst others flourish in a busier, more competitive group.

It's quite normal for babies and children to be a little upset at first by a new routine and new carers, especially when they have enjoyed the exclusive attention of their parents beforehand, but if the situation and the separation are handled sensitively, this should be minimal (see page 119). If, though, your baby or child cannot seem to settle into his new childcare arrangement after a period of several weeks, it may be that he is just not ready yet or that he would be happier after all with a different type of arrangement.

To help your baby or child over the separation, try following the steps given for the first question, 'How can I be sure my child will be happy?' Also, when it comes to the first time you need to leave your child, the best advice really is to go swiftly with a quick hug and a kiss and the reassurance that you will be back to collect him later (see page 160). Your own upbeat view of childcare, and your enthusiasm for it, will encourage your child to develop a similar perspective.

Q What if he won't behave himself?

A It's a psychological fact that normal behaviour in children can be challenging, and challenging behaviour can be normal. It's perfectly normal, for example, for a toddler to be reluctant to share his toys – he hasn't yet learnt this important social skill. It's also a normal part of a toddler's development to have tantrums, even very challenging ones, and they occur in virtually every child at some stage during the pre-school years. A good, experienced childcarer will realise that these types of difficult behaviour are part and parcel of social development.

If, on the other hand, your child's behaviour is not socially acceptable – if, for instance, he bites, kicks or hurts other children in any way – you may be asked to remove him temporarily from his childcare placement. Disruptive behaviour such as this is not usual in all children, and may mean that your child is under stress. Whether or not you have to take your child out of the childcare placement, you should discuss with his childcarer some strategies for correcting this behaviour, and agree an action plan between you for getting him back into childcare at a later date.

Q What if he loves his carer more than me?

A This is a very common worry amongst new parents, and one that illustrates how childcare can sometimes be a double-edged sword: we want our children to be as happy as possible, but not so delighted that they prefer someone else to us! One of the most important aspects of good childcare, however, is that a child feels loved and secure, and this can happen only if he is with someone he trusts and feels comfortable with – but this type of affection is not the same as the feelings he has for you, even if he seems to be rubbing your nose in his relationship with his carer!

Try to view any reluctance on your child's part to come home with you as a positive thing: after all, if he was running headlong towards you in tears or blaming you for leaving him in the first place, you would be sick with worry that he wasn't enjoying himself. Bear in mind that the relationship he has with his carer will be relatively short-lived compared with his relationship with you. Be prepared, too, for your child to use the childcarer as a 'higher authority' sometimes when it comes to challenging your ideas of discipline, especially in the early days. This is natural, and your child will soon learn not to play one adult off against another, especially if you make his childcarer aware of what's going on so you can work consistently together.

If you are concerned that your child and his carer are becoming so close that their relationship is likely to cause your child great upset when the time comes for it to end, that is a different matter: in this case, suggest a change of key worker if he's at a nursery, or try chatting it through with his childminder. How has she coped with this situation in the past? Could she perhaps transfer some of the attention she's giving your child to one of the other children in her care or encourage his interest in something absorbing? If things don't change, you will have to turn your attention towards making the break easier when the time comes. Perhaps you could reduce his hours in childcare over a few weeks before stopping it altogether – and perhaps he could leave when there's a natural break coming up, such as a family holiday, that he can look forward to.

Overall, childcare often enhances the parent-child relationship because parents value their time with their children more and make more of an effort to spend quality time together when they get the chance. In the majority of cases, fears that a child will develop a greater attachment to his carer than to his parents are unfounded and, in general, good-quality childcare should be a positive addition to the life of everyone in your family.

Q What if he won't eat?

A If your weaned baby or child is a particularly fussy eater and refuses the food his childcarer provides, it's wise to pack a few snacks from the list of foods he will eat to see him through the day. Make them as healthy as you can so that even if he eats very little, he is getting something nutritious. If he is still having baby milk, or if he enjoys cows' milk (full-fat up to age two, then full-fat or semi-skimmed until age five), you can rest assured that as long as he drinks around a pint (600 ml) a day, he will be getting sufficient calories and nutrients to survive. You'll need to ensure that he eats as well as possible when he's at home as he could become deficient in iron and other nutrients if he takes only milk.

A good nursery or childminder will encourage your baby or child to taste a variety of different foods. With toddlers and older children, this should not only be during mealtimes, but also during creative play or 'cookery' sessions as part of the early years curriculum. If a food is refused, it should be reintroduced again a few weeks later, and alternative foods offered until your child eventually expands the repertoire of foods he will eat. Children are very heavily influenced by peer pressure, and are more likely to try something new if they see another child eating it – in fact, many parents find that their children's eating habits improve in childcare rather than deteriorating. A nursery will probably not want to encourage children to bring packed lunches, as this will require extra storage facilities and perhaps expose other children to foods to which they might be allergic. A childminder, however, may be happy for you to provide your child's lunch, and you should negotiate terms so that you are not paying for foods your child is not having. If you are employing a nanny or au pair, unless your child willingly eats the foods she cooks, it may be worth cooking for the freezer or showing her how to prepare your child's favourite recipes.

If you remain very concerned about your baby's or child's refusal to eat solids, talk to your health visitor or GP. Not only will they be able to offer you further advice on broadening the range of foods your child will eat, but they will also keep close tabs on your child's physical development and may prescribe a nutritional supplement for him until things improve.

You and your childcarer

Q What if we disagree over discipline?

A This is really one of those matters to be ironed out during preliminary interviews, when it's fine to discuss how you can bring your discipline methods into line so that all parties concerned with your child's care are consistent. Sometimes, though, a child may report very different, undesirable behaviour by his carer than was discussed at the time. If this happens, try to get your child to explain in a little more detail what he is talking about before you confront your childminder: it may be that your child lacks the vocabulary to articulate things accurately. With any luck, you will find that there has been a misunderstanding, and your child's willingness or otherwise to resume childcare with his carer will give you some indication of this.

If you have reason to believe that your child's carer has disciplined him inappropriately (but without resorting to corporal punishment), find a good moment to talk at the nearest available opportunity, and voice your concerns. Ask her why she decided to deviate from your plan and give her a chance to explain. Be wary, though, if she tries to 'blame' your child: she is the adult and, as such, should be able to remain impassive and in charge at all times.

If, on the other hand, you have reason to believe that corporal punishment or threatening or abusive behaviour (including verbal abuse) has taken place, waste no time in removing your child from the care of that particular individual and reporting the incident to her employer, the local authority, the NSPCC or the police.

Q What if my child (or his carer) falls sick?

A The best plan is to have a fall-back arrangement in place, whether it means asking a relative or friend to be willing to step into the breach at short notice, or whether you sort out with your child's minder that they have contingency plans should the need arise.

If your childminder or nanny agency has alternative care ready and waiting should she herself be ill – and bear in mind that it is not her responsibility to provide this – you'll want to meet the back-up carer and vet her in the same way as you did your employed carer. Professional carers do often have their own networks and may be able to find an alternative if you can't.

If your child falls sick and is not able to attend nursery or go to his childminder for whatever reason, and you can't find a friend or relative to step into the breach, or if your own carer doesn't have a back-up waiting in the wings, you'll need to find another alternative. If you have a neighbour who uses a nanny, au pair, friend or relative, see if you could set up an emergency fall-back option between you where your child goes to their carer if he or his own carer is sick and vice versa.

If you use a nanny, ask at the agency whether or not they have emergency carers on stand-by to fill in for your permanent nanny. As a last resort, if there is no way that you or your partner can take time off work, you might find an agency nearby that specifically offers emergency cover. It will be costly, but could dig you out of a hole occasionally. Again, though, make sure you are very happy with the agency and the calibre of its staff before relying on this option. Try to source a potential agency through your local Childcare Information Services (visit www.childcarelink.gov.uk).

Q Should I leave my child in the care of a man?

A More and more men are entering the childcare sector, either as trained nannies or as childminders, but until it becomes commonplace, many parents – rightly or wrongly – are still a little suspicious about them. The same attitude is still sometimes in evidence towards male nurses and primary school teachers – in fact, amongst all professions that are traditionally dominated by females.

It's time to end the prejudice, as women have expected men to when they have entered predominantly male professions. As long as your potential childcarer – whether female or male – can provide you with the proper credentials and has been properly vetted, either by you or by the Criminal Records Bureau, there is no reason why a man should not do just as good a job as a woman. In fact, in single-parent families where the children are boys, some mothers find that having a positive male role model playing a large part in their sons' upbringing helps to bridge a gap that would otherwise be left unfilled – and this view is echoed by other families, too, regardless of whether or not there is a permanent father figure present.

Q Should I use a webcam to monitor my childcarer?

A Some nurseries may have webcams installed, whereby you can log on to a website and watch the children and staff at any time of the day. The onus is on the nursery to install this feature, however, and you won't be able to watch your child if they don't have the necessary equipment. The same goes for childminders.

Whether or not you install a webcam in your own home to watch what goes on between your child and his nanny, au pair or other home-based carer is up to you, but you should make the carer aware that you may be watching in via the internet at any time. It would be unsurprising if your childcarer showed some reluctance in agreeing to be watched and monitored remotely in this way: she will almost certainly feel that you are calling her capabilities and/or suitability as a childcarer into question, even if you couch the idea in terms of having greater contact with your children throughout the day. A compromise would be for you to agree between yourselves a couple of pre-arranged times during the day when you can watch and communicate with your child and his carer.

Ideally, the relationship of trust, coupled with good references or recommendations, your gut instinct and your own vetting procedures at the time of selecting your childcare provider, will mean that there is no need for a webcam.

You and your money

Q Can I get help with childcare costs?

A Probably. Depending on your financial circumstances, you may be eligible for help with the cost of childcare, either through Child Tax and Working Tax Credits or via Childcare Vouchers. Ninety per cent of families are eligible to claim tax credits.

Child Tax Credit is paid from the government directly into the bank account of the person who is mainly responsible for looking after your child. Families on a total income of up to £58,000 a year (or £66,000 in families where at least one child is less than a year old) can benefit from the Child Tax Credit regardless of whether they are working.

Working Tax Credit is a tax credit for employed families, which includes an element of support towards the costs of registered or approved childcare. In order for you to qualify for support, your childcare provider must be either a registered childminder, nursery, playscheme or out-of-school club; a school or other establishment that is exempt from being registered; a childcare provider for children aged eight or over who is approved by an accredited organisation or an approved home carer. In addition, if you are a lone parent, you must work for at least 16 hours per week; if you are part of a couple, you must both work for at least 16 hours per week, unless one of you is incapacitated, in which case the other must work for at least 16 hours per week.

The childcare element of the Working Tax Credit will pay a sliding scale of up to 80% of the costs of eligible childcare to a maximum of £122.50 per week for one child and £210 per week for two or more children. Monies are paid directly into the bank account of the main carer.

For more information, or for help with completing your claim form, call the Tax Credit helpline on 0845 300 3900 (or 0845 300 3909 if you have speech or hearing difficulties and you live in England, Scotland or Wales). To apply online, or to find out whether or not you are eligible, visit www.hmrc.gov.uk/taxcredits.

Your employer may help you with childcare costs, saving both you and your employer money, through tax and National Insurance Contributions (NICs) exemptions. There are three schemes enabling employers to do this:

1. Your employer can provide you with childcare vouchers of up to £55 per week (£243 per month), which you then redeem with your childcare provider.
2. Your employer can make payments directly to your childcare provider – up to £55 per week (£243 per month).
3. Your employer can provide childcare in the workplace to the value of the full amount of the usual childcare subsidy, leaving you liable for any outstanding costs.

The exemption means that employees pay neither income tax nor National Insurance contributions on the support, and employers pay no National Insurance contributions.

For further information on schemes to support childcare costs, contact Daycare Trust (www.daycaretrust.org.uk).

Q I'm currently on maternity leave and want to go back to work part time. Where do I stand with my employer?

A You have the right to request to return to your job – or a similar position with the same pay and benefits (pro rata), level of seniority and promotion prospects – either part time, or to any other working pattern of your choice, but this doesn't give you an automatic entitlement to flexible working. Your employer does have a statutory duty to give your proposal serious consideration. If your request is refused, however, your employer will be legally obliged to produce written evidence that your proposed working pattern is not practicable or would be detrimental to the business. For more information, contact the Department of Trade & Industry on 020 7215 5000 or visit www.dti.gov.uk.

Q How do I sort out my nanny's tax, National Insurance Contributions and payslips?

A This can be complicated, and you will probably need to register as an employer and operate a PAYE (Pay As You Earn) scheme, so contact the Inland Revenue to find out more details. By far the easiest solution, if you can afford it, is to put these matters in the hands of a reputable agency, which can not only calculate tax and National Insurance Contributions, but can also raise a payslip detailing the monetary breakdown. This will cost you around £20 per month or £250 per year (or less if you nanny-share, as you and the other family will share costs).

You as a working parent

Q I'm worried about getting the balance right between working and spending time with my child. How can I approach this so that no one suffers?

A It's the common cry of nearly all working parents, especially where the main carer is returning to work. How well you handle the transition back to work may be influenced in part by how motivated you are to return to your job: if you are unhappy about working, you are more likely to allow that discontentment to filter through to the rest of your family. If, on the other hand, you have a genuine desire to return to the workplace, your own fulfilment can have a very positive knock-on effect.

Either way, the early days of working after having a baby are likely to prove challenging. As time goes on, however, you'll find that you settle into your new pattern and learn to be even more flexible, finding strategies to cope with upsets to the routine, and juggling your work-life balance until you find the right set-up for the whole family.

Here are some pointers to help you and your child get the very best out of your working-mum status:

- Make a point of setting aside specific times of the day when you can spend one-to-one time with your baby or child. This could be first thing in the morning during a feed or breakfast, as soon as you return home, or just before bedtime. Ideally, try to do something together at each of these regular times.

- Have some special activities planned that are just for the two of you to share: perhaps reading a particular book, playing with your child's favourite toy, sharing a bath, making a weekly trip to the play park, or watching a much-loved DVD together.
- Don't forget to plan 'family time' into your week, especially at the weekends. It's hard to find prolonged periods when you're a working parent, as spare time tends to get allocated to household maintenance, shopping or cleaning – but try to find an hour or so every so often to play together (without the distraction of TV or music), share a meal, go to the cinema, or have a lovely walk. This will help you to build lasting memories you can all treasure.
- Start your own family traditions: these can build into wonderful memories that act as landmarks down the years, and they also provide a sense of consistency and continuity for your child. Some families regularly share some of their week's experiences over Sunday lunch, for example; others have a family photo session once a month. Perhaps you could enjoy a takeaway with a particular family TV programme each week, or share a bedtime story between all of you on specific evenings.
- Try to leave your work at work: make an effort to switch off from any work-related stress (even positive stress) when you come home to your child. Focus on his day and what he has achieved; sing to your young baby and play 'Peep-o' with him; talk in a soothing voice. You'll notice that in engaging with your baby or child, you wind down and relax

yourself, so you could regard it as a kind of 'family therapy'! Similarly, stick to your working hours strictly: if you don't work on Thursdays, for instance, don't start accepting phone calls or checking emails from home on Thursdays. If you treat your home time as sacrosanct, so will other people.

- Focus on quality rather than quantity when it comes to shared time together. Try to ignore any minor undesirable behaviour in your child, and praise him for any effort he makes to please you. Make allowances, too, for some disruption to his behaviour patterns when you take over from his childcarer: he may have made a big effort to be a 'good boy' all day, for example, only to want to give vent to a few frustrations in the safe environment of home and Mummy or Daddy.
- Accept that you may not be a superstar either at work or at home for a while. By splitting your time between your employer and your family, you won't have 100% to give to either, but remind yourself that you are making a valuable contribution to work whilst giving the best attention you can to your child.

Q I have feelings of guilt and jealousy when I hear full-time mums talking about all the things they manage to do with their kids every day. How can I overcome them?

A Remember that, whether through choice or necessity, you are doing your best for your family. Consider, too, that many stay-at-home mums also have feelings of guilt, but that theirs are around not providing materially for the family. Some also suffer from jealousy of working mums, who may seem to enjoy the 'best of both worlds'. For this and other reasons, some women may well 'talk up' their new, full-time mum roles in order to make themselves feel better, but in reality the picture is unlikely to be rosy all the time.

If, however, you're feeling bad because you think you have made a wrong choice or you are not spending enough time with your child, you could reconsider your options: perhaps your partner could work more flexibly; perhaps you could reassess your childcare arrangements; maybe you could afford to cut your hours at the expense of a few luxuries?

There is no right or wrong answer to the question of whether parents should go out to work. There is also no such thing as a perfect parent. As long as your baby or child has a strong bond of attachment to you, and as long as you enjoy the time you spend together (for the most part!) and have achieved a balance that you are reasonably happy with, congratulate yourself – you're doing a great job, at work and at home.

Useful contacts

Telephone numbers are supplied wherever available. Some organisations are contactable only online.

Best Bear Childcare
A company that provides a comprehensive and quality-controlled guide to childcare agencies across the UK, designed to help parents make informed decisions.

Tel: 08707 201277
www.bestbear.co.uk

Care Standards Inspectorate for Wales (CSIW)
If you live in Wales and cannot resolve a problem between you and your carer, or you wish to make an official complaint about inappropriate behaviour, you can contact this organisation.

Tel: 029 2047 8600
www.csiw.wales.gov.uk

Childcare Approval Scheme (CAS)
A voluntary scheme run by the DfES for carers who are not required to be registered by Ofsted. Its aims are to raise the standard of home-based care and allow greater numbers of parents to access financial support. The scheme applies only to childcare provided in England.

Tel: 0845 767 8111
www.childcareapprovalscheme.co.uk

ChildcareLink
A government service offering information and advice on childcare.

Tel: 0800 096 0296
www.childcarelink.gov.uk

Children's Information Services
(*see* National Association of Children's Information Services)

Children's Workforce Development Council (CWDC)
Exists to improve the lives of children, young people, their families and carers by ensuring that all people working with them have the best possible training, qualifications, support and advice.

Tel: 0113 244 6311
www.cwdcouncil.org.uk

Daycare Trust
A national childcare charity that promotes high-quality affordable childcare for all. Its hotline offers free information and advice for parents.

Tel: 020 7840 3350
www.daycaretrust.org.uk

Department for Education and Skills (DfES)
The government department that deals with all aspects of education, although childcare and pre-school provision up to age three are dealt with by the Department of Health. The DfES website gives full details of the Effective Provision of Pre-school Education (EPPE) Project.

www.dfes.gov.uk

Department of Trade & Industry (DTI)

This government department offers information about your employment and maternity rights.

Tel: 020 7215 5000
www.dti.gov.uk

Directgov
The government's public services network. It provides information from across UK government departments on topics ranging from travel safety and parental leave to special educational needs and local NHS services.

www.direct.gov.uk

Discovery Home & Health
A satellite television channel dealing with matters relating to home, health, lifestyle and family. Its website offers useful discussion forums.

www.homeandhealthtv.co.uk

Employers for Childcare
A registered charity that helps working parents in Northern Ireland to find childcare solutions. It also provides practical advice about work, family and finances.

Tel: 0800 028 3008
www.employersforchildcare.org

Grandparents Association
A group that offers support and advice to grandparents who have lost or are losing contact with their grandchildren because of divorce, family feud or other problems; are caring for their grandchildren on a full-time basis; have childcare responsibilities for their grandchildren; or are interested in the educational and welfare needs of their grandchildren.

Tel: 0845 4349585
www.grandparents-association.org.uk

Investors in Children (IiC)
(*see* Sure Start website)

National Association of Children's Information Services (NACIS)
Offering guidance to families, childcare providers and employers on a range of issues related to raising a family. Local branches hold lists of all registered childcare provision in the area.

Tel: 020 7515 9000
www.nacis.org.uk

National Childbirth Trust (NCT)
A leading UK charity for pregnancy, birth and parenting, offering information, reassurance and support.

Tel: 0870 444 8707
www.nct.org.uk

National Childminding Association (NCMA)
The umbrella body for registered childminders in England and Wales. Working in partnership with the government, it offers lots of useful information about finding and vetting the appropriate carer for your child.

Tel: 0845 880 0044
www.ncma.org.uk

National Day Nurseries Association (NDNA)
The umbrella body for registered day nurseries. It aims to enhance the development and education of children in their early years through the provision of support services to members.

Tel: 0870 774 4244
www.ndna.org.uk

National Society for the Prevention of Cruelty to Children (NSPCC)
A long-established charity that deals with all aspects of child abuse.

Tel: 0808 800 5000
www.nspcc.org.uk

Netmums
A discussion forum that offers mums, dads and anyone else working with families a wealth of information and advice. Regional branches offer local information and support.

www.netmums.com

Northern Ireland Childminding Association (NICMA)
If you live in Northern Ireland and cannot resolve a problem between you and your carer, or you wish to make an official complaint about inappropriate behaviour, you can contact this organisation.

Tel: 028 9181 1015
www.nicma.org

Office for Standards in Education (Ofsted)
If you live in England and cannot resolve a problem between you and your carer, or you wish to make an official complaint about inappropriate behaviour, you can contact this organisation.

Tel: 0845 601 4772
www.ofsted.gov.uk

Parentline Plus
A national charity that works for, and with, parents. It offers help and support through an innovative range of free, flexible, responsive services – shaped by parents for parents.

Tel: 0808 800 2222
www.parentlineplus.org.uk

Pre-school Learning Alliance (PLA)
A leading educational charity that provides practical support to community pre-schools. Its products and services include specialist publications, directly managed childcare provision, information and advice, quality assurance, campaigning, research, training and family programmes.

Tel: 020 7697 2500
www.pre-school.org.uk

Scottish Commission for the Regulation of Care (SCRC)
If you live in Scotland and cannot resolve a problem between you and your carer, or you wish to make an official complaint about inappropriate behaviour, you can contact this organisation.

Tel: 01382 207100

www.carecommission.com

Sure Start
A government programme (run as a unit within the DfES, see page 178) that aims to deliver the best start in life for every child. It brings together early education, childcare, health and family support.

www.surestart.gov.uk

Tax Credit helpline
For help and information, or to find out if you are eligible, contact HM Revenue & Customs.

Tel: 0845 300 3900
www.hmrc.gov.uk/taxcredits

UK Parents
A discussion forum where parents can discuss anything relating to children and families.

www.ukparents.co.uk

Working Families
The UK's leading work-life balance organisation. Offers help and advice to working parents, carers and employers.

Tel: 020 7253 7243
www.workingfamilies.org.uk

Other sources of information

Your local phone book – just look under the appropriate heading.

Your local library – nurseries and other childcare providers sometimes advertise on its noticeboard.

Your health visitor or doctor – they sometimes keep a list of nurseries and other childcare.

Your employer – there may be a workplace nursery for employees' use.

Other parents – a great source because nothing beats a personal recommendation.

Online – nanny and au pair agencies can be found online, as well as in phone books. Remember, though, that it's down to you to make checks that these companies are reputable and bona fide, especially as the staff on their books will be unregistered.

Index